SHIP STRIKE PACIFIC

John R. Bruning Jr.

ZENITH
PRESS

Dedication

This one's for Jenn. Without you, I'd be lost.

First published in 2005 by Zenith Press, an imprint of MBI Publishing Company, Galtier Plaza, Suite 200, 380 Jackson Street, St. Paul, MN 55101-3885 USA

Zenith Press titles are also available at discounts in bulk quantity for industrial or sales-promotional use. For details write to Special Sales Manager at MBI Publising Company, Galtier Plaza, Suite 200, 380 Jackson Street, St. Paul, MN 55101-3885 USA.

ISBN 0-7603-2095-0

Editorial: Lindsay Hitch
Design: Kari Johnston

Printed in China

On the frontispiece:
By the early spring of 1945, the Fifth Air Force had redeployed its medium bomber force to Luzon, where the B-25s were used against convoys off the China coast. In late March and early April, the 345th Bomb Group attacked and virtually destroyed two such convoys. This image shows the convoy off Swatow, China, under attack by the Air Apaches.

On the title page:
After the 5th Air Force's successes with modified strafer Mitchells, units across the Pacific and China Burma India (CBI) Theater made similar changes to their aircraft. This photo shows six .50-caliber machine guns installed in the nose of a 341st Bomb Group B-25 in the CBI.

On the back cover:
In 1943, the Fifth Air Force's B-25 crews joined the ship-killer ranks with a vengeance. Rearmed with field-modified Mitchells, they employed new masthead attack tactics that decimated the Japanese sea lanes in the Southwest Pacific Area. Here, a Fifth Air Force plane roars past a Japanese antisubmarine escort off Kavieng as a cargo ship burns in the background. Note the bomb bouncing off the water at the bottom of the photo.

About the Author
John Bruning earned a B.A. in History from the University of Oregon in 1990. While in graduate school at the U of O, he served as the aviation historian for Dyanmix Inc.'s award-winning historical flight simulation team, where he worked on Red Baron, Aces of the Pacific, and Aces over Europe, and designed Red Baron II. He left Dynamix in 1996 to pursue a career in writing and consulting. Bruning is currently the author of five books and numerous articles, and he has consulted on a broad range of historical projects ranging from documentaries and museum projects to multi-media CD-Rom software titles. Bruning lives in Independence, Oregon, with his wife Jennifer, son Eddie, and daughter Renee.

Contents

Acknowledgments

This book would not have been possible without considerable help from many people. At the top of the list are Eric Hammel and Richard Kane. Without their support of this project, *Ship Strike Pacific* never would have seen the light of day. To both of you I owe a debt of sincere gratitude. And to Eric, my friend and mentor: you are my ambassador of Quan, baby!

The many veterans who have shared their memories with me over the last 14 years provided many of the details included within these covers. They include: General John Henebry, Sumner Whitten, Bill Runey, Stanley "Swede" Vejtasa, Ken Ruiz, Dewey Ray, Ted Crosby, Jack DeTour, Harry Ferrier, Bruce Williams, Larry Cauble, and many others.

A special thanks goes out to David Aiken, who is the leading expert on the tactical aspects of the Pearl Harbor attack. Without his help and support, the first chapter would not have been complete.

I owe a huge debt of gratitude to Kate Flaherty, Holly Reed, and Theresa Roy at the Still Pictures Branch of the National Archives. Without their assistance, this book would never have been possible. A special thanks also goes to the folks at the Hoover Archives for their help and guidance.

My family's unyielding support helped get me through many late nights as I worked to complete the book. My son, Eddie, sat with me through many sessions as I selected photographs and wrote captions. He's probably the only three-year-old in the world who can identify almost every American and Japanese aircraft used in the Pacific War. His grandparents are convinced he'll need years of therapy to overcome my parenting. They may be right!

My daughter, Renee, served as my research assistant, working the microfilm copier at Western Oregon University like a pro. She also assisted in keeping her old man organized and convinced me to take a break every now and then so that she might blow me up in Halo on Xbox—just to keep a little perspective. Rocket launchers are a girl's best friend.

Denice and Andy Scott, thanks for your patience as I spent mornings at Andy's Cafe taking notes for each chapter. This book was fueled by your eggs and hash browns! If you're ever in my part of the world, this is the best place on the West Coast for breakfast.

To Debra Goldstein and Emily Pullins, words are not enough to express how much your loyalty and friendship altered my life. I would not be the person I am today without the two of you.

I wrote my first book in the basement of the local museum. It proved to be haunted, so I moved a block over into an old Odd Fellow's Lodge. Thanks to Bob and Laura Archer for providing such an interesting place for my office. When they bought the building some years ago, it came complete with a coffin and skeleton, a leftover artifact from its days as an Odd Fellow's Lodge. No ghosts, though.

Lastly, I'd like to thank my close friend Jack Cook. Jack's mind is a marvel—a true encyclopedia of aviation knowledge gleaned from 30 years of study and friendships with the men who fought in World War II. His assistance has proven invaluable time and again. I know you hate my sappy intros, pal, but you are my best friend. Thanks for everything.

THOSE WHO SHAPED HISTORY

ARE THE CURRENTS OF HISTORY SO STRONG THAT ONE MAN OR WOMAN CANNOT INFLUENCE THEIR COURSE?

The "Great Man" theory of history has long since fallen out of vogue in academic circles. Instead, academic historians search for other reasons why human events have taken the form they have. Some look at societal reasons. Others look to gender and race.

These days, individual achievement is suborned to the idea that history is so multifaceted and tremendous in scope that it moves forward on the momentum of ages.

But what of the decisions of Lee and Grant, Foch and Haig, Wilson? How does this concept of history allow for Yamamoto and his radical idea to attack Pearl Harbor? Without his willingness to stake his career on that one raid, the scar of that terrible Sunday would not linger in the American psyche. And what of Douglas MacArthur and his pledge to return to the Philippines? Without his oratorical skills, would FDR have listened to the navy and bypassed the islands instead? What radical changes that would have brought for the Filipinos and the postwar relationship between our two nations.

To deny that the power to change human events can reside in a few men and women is to fundamentally misunderstand the nature of military history. But the act is understandable given how little military history is taught in American universities today.

I am old school. I believe in the Great Man theory, but with an added corollary. There are times when a confluence of events, technology, and individuals create the rarest of opportunities—the chance for an ordinary human to play a tremendous role in how his time is shaped. Who can deny the effect the 19-year-old student-turned-assassin Gavrilo Princip had on Europe? Did he die in prison burdened by guilt for the war he sparked and the millions claimed by it? Or what of Franz Ferdinand's driver who, lost in an unfamiliar city, took a wrong turn that brought the Archduke face-to-face with his young assassin? Had he made the right turn, perhaps there may have been no war in 1914. By accident or design, ordinary people can change the fate of nations.

Nowhere is this more evident than in the early months of the Pacific War. When the issue hung in the balance as both Japan and America sought to control the strategic flow of the war, the bomber crew emerged as the great catalyst for change. These twenty-something kids, fresh from college dances and happier times at home, found themselves suddenly thrust to center stage in a conflict so vast they were but a leaf in a storm. Blown to the farthest reaches of the planet, their country put them in harm's way and vested in them hope that their skill and bravery would stem the tide of Japanese aggression.

The Japanese defined the strategic nature of the Pacific War on December 7, 1941, when they proved the supremacy of aircraft over the capital ship. That old scourge of the sea, the battleship, could be turned to so much scrap metal by only a few air-launched torpedoes. The aircraft, as an offensive instrument of naval power, had arrived.

This revolution in warfare spawned a new kind of warrior, the ship-killer. It was here that ordinary men shined. One pilot, one crew, could strike a blow that altered the strategic balance in the Pacific. Men such as Murata, Ault, Larner, Henebry, and others scored battle-changing hits in the course of their anti-ship missions. These men—these twenty-somethings—determined the flow of events with their courage and skill. They became the ship-killers, and history rode with them in their cockpits.

The ship-killers paid the price. Attacking ships was perhaps the most difficult aerial mission of World War II. Ships were high-value targets, and thus heavily defended. Time after time, raiding squadrons were shot out of the sky. The destruction of Torpedo Eight at Midway was a symbol, not an aberration.

When the war was over and the survivors returned home, historians gave them the shaft. The commentators of the Pacific Air War devoted reams of print to the exploits of the fighter jocks. The aces represented freedom; their stories filled with wild melees and individual triumph. The bomber crews, the men who really dictated the course of the Pacific War, sank into anonymity. Today, while the battles they won are well-known—Pearl Harbor, Midway, Leyte Gulf—the crews themselves have all but been forgotten. It is a cruel irony of history that these men who did so much to shape our world have been obscured with the passage of years. It is also a grave injustice and the reason for this book.

Ship Strike Pacific examines some of the most important air-sea actions of World War II. Some are well-known, some nearly forgotten. Some of these attacks proved stunningly successful, others ended in total failure. In each case, brave photographers had the presence of mind to document these engagements so that future generations could see with their own eyes what these men achieved in the remote corners of the Pacific.

This book is their story.

Chapter One

How 40 Men Destroyed the U.S. Navy's Pacific Battle Line

ARISING SUN BROKE ACROSS THE EASTERN HORIZON—

dawn in the North Pacific. Among the heavy swells, six aircraft carriers bobbed like corks in a bathtub. These six and their attendant battleships, cruisers, and destroyers, known as the Kido Butai, had braved the violent winter sea with cold calculation. Rough weather, rough seas meant few ships would ply these waters at this time of year. The task force might slip unnoticed to its destination and strike a blow that would resound through history.

It was 0600, December 7, 1941, Hawaii time. Only a short time before, the six flat-tops had swung their bows into the wind. The decks pitched in the swells, and Vice Admiral Chuichi Nagumo, the force commander, feared that the conditions would slow the launch. Six-foot swells and a 28-knot northeasterly wind made the flight decks unpleasant places for everyone. As the sun rose, the conditions improved and the swells flattened out enough to ease the strain for the deck and air crews.

(opposite) In 1941, no navy possessed a better air arm than the Japanese. And while their equipment possessed deficiencies that would later prove very costly, the aircrews more than compensated with élan and experience. Fighting the Nationalist Chinese throughout the 1930s, the Japanese Naval Air Force's aircrews ranked among the most combat-savvy veterans in the world at that time.

(right) Admiral Chuichi Nagumo, the commander of the Imperial Japanese Navy's carrier task force (known as the Kido Butai), was worried that the heavy seas would cause problems during the launch of the first wave. As a result, he ordered it to begin earlier than had been originally scheduled.

The seas that morning caused the carriers to pitch and roll. The torpedo-armed Kates had to time their takeoff rolls perfectly in sync so they'd be airborne at the crest of a wave and well away from the ship once the deck began pitching down again. Here, a B5N waddles aloft just as the deck begins to drop. Another Kate, already airborne, is in the distance.

The moment had come. One by one, 183 aircraft rumbled down the wooden decks and waddled aloft, each heavily laden with fuel and ordnance. By 0630, the entire force had formed up and was heading south—south for Pearl Harbor.

The Pacific War, so characterized by air-sea engagements, was about to begin with one gigantic hammer blow from the sky directed squarely at the American Pacific Fleet.

While the initial wave of aircraft totaled almost 200 planes, 40 Nakajima B5N "Kate" bombers formed the mailed fist of the Japanese striking force. Armed with modified Type 91 Torpedoes re-engineered for use in shallow waters, these 40 planes composed the heart of the Pearl Harbor attack plan. The Kate crews were to destroy the battleships and carriers moored around Ford Island. Carriers *Hiryu*'s and *Soryu*'s B5Ns would target anything on the north side of Ford Island, while the elite crews from the *Akagi* and *Kaga* would swing around the harbor, turn north, and hit the battleships moored on the other side. Designed as a simultaneous pincher attack against the two key locations in the harbor, the Japanese pinned their hopes on these 40 crews and the damage they could inflict with their 1,764-pound torpedoes.

The entire plan revolved around this single element of the attack. If the Japanese achieved complete surprise over Oahu that morning, the plan called for the torpedo-armed Kates to go in first. Hopefully undetected, they would sweep into the harbor, deliver the knock-out blows, and escape before the American air defenses had time to react. Minutes later, the 51 Aichi D3A Val dive bombers from the *Zuikaku* and *Shokaku* would hit ground installations and airfields around the harbor, suppressing any American reaction to the attack. As the D3As went about their work, 49 B5N Kates from the *Akagi, Kaga, Hiryu,* and *Soryu* would make level bombing runs on the surviving capital ships in the harbor using modified 1,800-pound 16-inch naval shells as their weapons.

But, if surprise were not achieved, the Japanese intended to send all their aircraft in simultaneously so the torpedo-armed Kates would not face the full brunt of the American air defenses alone.

About 90 minutes after takeoff, the Japanese strike group went feet dry at Kahuku Point, the northernmost tip of Oahu. It was here that the first of many communication failures took place, all of which collectively served to soften the blow the Japanese delivered against the United States that morning.

Over Oahu, the skies were empty of American planes. No anti-aircraft fire greeted them, and the bases within view of the Japanese strike force looked quiet. They had achieved complete surprise. At 0749, Mitsuo Fuchida signaled his men. One Black Dragon flare arced high over the Japanese planes. Fired from Fuchida's aircraft, it was the order that was supposed to send the torpedo bombers in first. Surprise was theirs, now the Kates needed to make the most of it.

Fuchida looked around at his men. Nearby, a formation of A6M2 Zero fighters clung protectively to the skirt-tails of the bomber groups. Their job was to keep the American interceptors off the Kates and Vals or strafe the airfields if no aircraft greeted them. Leading the escorting Zeroes was the *Akagi*'s A6M squadron commander, Lieutenant Commander Shigeru Itaya. Fuchida studied his aircraft and concluded Itaya hadn't seen the Black Dragon flare. He fired another one right at his fighter leader's plane.

The second flare caused confusion in the bomber formations. Seeing the second flare, some of the pilots and flight leaders believed Fuchida had just signaled them that surprise had *not* been achieved. That second flare sent the strike groups into a pell-mell rush for their targets. Everyone would go in at once.

In fact, the suppressing Vals and strafing Zeroes made the initial attacks on the outlying bases around Pearl Harbor. The slower torpedo-armed Kates took several more minutes to reach their objectives.

Leading the torpedo attack that morning was the *Akagi*'s air group commander, Lieutenant Commander Shigeharu Murata. His second in command was Lieutenant Hiratu Matsumura, the B5N squadron leader from the *Hiryu*. Once the dive bombers, fighters, and bomb-armed Kates swung toward their targets, Murata led his formation down the coast to Waialua Bay and turned south toward the Waianae Mountains. It was here that his formation broke into two subgroups. The *Akagi*'s and *Kaga*'s 24 B5Ns stayed on the west side of the mountains, while Matsumura took the *Hiryu*'s and *Soryu*'s 16 Kates down the eastern side of the Waianae Range.

The Kates moved into attack formation—squadron strings with 500-yard intervals between each aircraft. But this follow-the-leader formation disrupted communications further. Nobody could see the hand signals their section or flight leaders used, and the confusion began to cause problems. With the *Hiryu*'s and *Soryu*'s Kates, the sun shined directly into their eyes, blotting out their view of much of the harbor. At the same time, attacking Val dive bombers struck Ford Island, setting a hangar afire. Unable to see his targets, Matsumura swung right and headed south, while *Soryu*'s eight planes continued on

directly into the harbor. The mailed fist had fragmented.

The confusion worsened when several of Matsumura's squadron mates missed his turn and lost track of him. They orbited over Ewa until they found Lieutenant Hiroharu Kadono, the *Hiryu*'s B5N squadron executive officer. He gathered up his scattered planes and led them into the harbor behind Matsumura. The attack would go in piecemeal.

Meanwhile, as the *Soryu*'s and *Hiryu*'s Kates stumbled toward the harbor, Murata's men stayed with him as he led them over Ewa Mooring Mast Field at 1,500 feet. At that point, he swung south and took them out over the coast. Once he reached the beach, Murata banked left and dove for the entrance to Pearl Harbor.

While Murata and his section leader kept their six Kates together in parallel trail formations about 100 yards apart, the other six *Akagi* Kates became spread out by all the

Battleship row under attack. These ships were the target of Japan's best carrier attack pilots. Ships from left to right are: battleships *Nevada*, *Arizona* with the repair ship *Vestal* alongside her, *West Virginia*, *Tennessee*, *Oklahoma*, and *Maryland*; fleet oiler *Neosho*; and the *California* moored by herself. Here, the attack has just commenced, and torpedo tracks head for the ships. The *West Virginia* and *Oklahoma* have already been hit by Lieutenant (jg) Jinichi Goto and Lieutenant Commander Shigeharu Murata's flight of six *Akagi* B5Ns. In the background, smoke issues from *Oglala* and *Helena* alongside the 1010 dock, victim of Lieutenant Tyoshi Nagai's torpedo attack. Further in the distance, more smoke and flames virtually obscure Hickam Field. At the end of the 1010 dock, the USS *Argonne* can faintly be seen. It was aboard that ship that some of the most telling film and still images of the attack on battleship row were taken.

maneuvering. Instead of 500 yards between each aircraft, the intervals opened to 1,500 to 1,800 yards. The same happened to the *Kaga's* 12 Kates. The spacing would have a drastic effect on these final planes attacking battleship row.

Murata and his men reached the harbor just before 0800. The attack had already been under way for several minutes, and as he dropped down to 60 feet and slowed to 160 knots to allow for the best possible drop, American anti-aircraft fire was already streaming toward him and his men.

Murata selected the battleship *West Virginia* as his target. He led his two wingmen down onto the stationary ship and released his torpedo. Behind him, Airman 1st Class Fujuki Murakami bored in and dropped his fish as well. But Murata's number three, Airman 1st Class Sadasuke Katsuki suddenly veered left. Instead of staying on the *West Virginia* with the rest of his flight, he changed course and drove hard for the *Oklahoma*.

Katsuki veered right into the parallel string of three more *Akagi* Kates, led by Lieutenant (jg) Jinichi Goto. Goto had led his men against the *Oklahoma* at the same time Murata's flight was going after the *West Virginia*. He and his number two wingman released and came off target, but just as his number three, Airman 1st Class Tomoe Yasue, lined up for his attack, Katsuki nearly collided with him. Yasue jettisoned his torpedo and pulled back hard on his stick. His Kate leapt skyward just as Katsuki's plane sliced underneath him. It had been a near miss, and Katsuki's mistake cost the attack group a torpedo.

Nevertheless, Murata's initial attack succeeded. Torpedoes slammed home into both the *West Virginia* and the *Oklahoma*, and the ships reeled from their lethal impact.

The battlewagons would gain no respite as the first Kates pulled up and headed for home. Behind them came the second group of six *Akagi* planes in a ragged, elongated double trail.

Minutes into the torpedo attack, this scene was captured from a Japanese aircraft from the north side of Ford Island. At left are the secondary targets many of the *Soryu's* Kates attacked. Closest to the camera is the training battleship *Utah*, followed by the light cruisers USS *Raleigh* and USS *Detroit*. USS *Raleigh* is already listing, hit by Tatsumi Nakajima's torpedo. In the background, battleship row can be seen under attack. A geyser of water, probably from a torpedo hit, has sprouted alongside USS *West Virginia*. Overhead are two Japanese aircraft, probably D3A Vals assigned to attack Ford Island.

Meanwhile, on the other side of Ford Island, the *Hiryu's* and *Soryu's* Kates reached the harbor in small clusters. The first group, led by the hard-charging Lieutenant Tyoshi Nagai from the *Soryu*, broke to starboard over the Middle Loch and pointed their Kates straight for the moorings on the north side of Ford Island. But as Nagai closed the range, he realized there weren't any worthwhile targets. The American carriers usually moored on this side of Ford Island, but on this Sunday morning, with the flat-tops at sea delivering aircraft to Midway and Wake, the training battleship *Utah* and two aging light cruisers had taken their places.

Nagai had to make a decision. He could either press his attack or break it off in the face of increasingly heavy anti-aircraft fire and find another target. An experienced commander, he searched for another target he could reach quickly. Over to his right, Nagai saw what appeared to be a gigantic battleship alongside the 1010 dock. That would be his target. He aborted his run and swung his nose to starboard.

Behind him, the sudden turn caused more confusion. The second group of four *Soryu* Kates stayed on target, led by Tatsumi Nakajima. Two of Nagai's wingmen turned and joined Nakajima's attack. Consequently, six of the eight planes from *Soryu*'s torpedo group had broken ranks to make runs at secondary targets at best. It was a mistake that outraged Nagai's number two, Juzo Mori, who resolved to not waste his weapon on such unworthy targets. He sped on and over Ford Island, intent on getting to battleship row.

As Mori struck out on his own, Nakajima dropped on the *Utah*, but in the excitement of the moment he'd released from too sharp an angle. The weapon surged past the training ship and struck the light cruiser *Raleigh*. The blast tore a hole below the armored belt so large that it flooded two boiler rooms and the forward engine room. A list developed that almost caused the ship to capsize, and only some very creative damage control saved the old CL.

Nakajima's three trailing wingmen attacked the *Utah*. One of the torpedoes remains unaccounted for, one struck the shoreline near the light cruiser *Detroit*, while the fish fired by Airman 1st Class Karoku Fujiwara struck the *Utah*. The two strays from Nagai's flight also released. One hit the *Utah* while the other exploded against the shoreline near the listing *Raleigh*. The hits doomed the old training ship, which rolled over and sank into the harbor mud. Along with the *Arizona*, it is the only ship remaining today in the harbor that was sunk during the attack.

The attacks on this side of Ford Island failed to have much strategic value. The six Kate crews squandered their torpedoes on warships of only minimal value. Had those torpedoes been brought around the other side of the harbor and used against the *California* or *Nevada*, the destruction wrought on those two ships could have rivaled what happened to *West Virginia* and *Oklahoma*, possibly even knocking them out of the war. It was a mistake the Japanese themselves recognized both during and after the attack.

The *Hiryu*'s strike group did only slightly better. Disorganized even before they reached the harbor, the fragmented formations splintered further as some of the pilots attacked the *Utah* with Nakajima's *Soryu* group. Others followed the *Soryu*'s lead pilot, Nagai, against the 1010 dock.

Nagai closed the range on his 1010 dock target, believing he was about to strike a battleship. But the ship in his sights turned out to be no battleship. Instead, he had selected the modern light cruiser *Helena*, which was berthed alongside an ancient minelayer, USS *Oglala*. The combined silhouette of the two ships caused the *Hiryu*'s pilots to misidentify them as a single battleship.

Nagai pressed his attack and dropped his torpedo, even as intense anti-aircraft fire began splattering around him from the battleship *Pennsylvania*, which lay in dry dock nearby. His torpedo arrowed right under the *Oglala* and struck the *Helena*. The blow delivered a vicious blast that ruptured the *Oglala*'s eggshell hull. With no way to control the flooding, the minelayer began to roll over onto the *Helena*. Recognizing the danger, the *Helena* crew managed to move their stricken ship out of the way. The *Oglala* ultimately rolled over onto the 1010 dock and came to rest on her side.

Behind Nagai, four more *Hiryu* Kate pilots dropped on the *Helena* and *Oglala*. None of those torpedoes hit. Stiff anti-aircraft fire now greeted each attacker, and several were hit. One Kate was holed 29 times during the course of the attack, but the crew still managed to drop its weapon at 200 yards and return to the *Hiryu*.

Two of the remaining *Hiryu* Kate crews realized Nagai had just attacked a cruiser. They aborted their run at the 1010 dock and arched around Ford Island to go after battleship row. In the process, they flew into the middle of the onrushing Kates from the *Akagi*'s second flight of six just in time to join into the climactic attack on battleship row.

Fortified with strays from the strike on the other side of Ford Island, the second half of the *Akagi*'s squadron skimmed the water of the Southeast Loch and began selecting targets. With *West Virginia* and *Oklahoma* already hit and gushing oil from their punctured hulls, the first three pilots picked out the undamaged *California* as their target. Lieutenant Asao Negishi and Petty Officer 3rd Class Gunji Kaido successfully released on the lone battleship moored some distance away from her cohorts. Behind them, however, flak tore into Airman 1st Class Keigo Hanai's B5N, mortally wounding one of his crewmen. He broke off his run and turned for the *West Virginia*. He dropped his torpedo and was able to get his stricken plane back to the *Akagi*.

Negishi and Kaido were outstanding attack pilots. One, and possibly both, torpedoes struck the *California*. The damage inflicted proved to be severe and was compounded by many open manholes that prevented the ship from achieving complete watertight integrity. Water began pouring into the big battlewagon, prompting a list that peaked at 16 degrees before counter-flooding successfully controlled it. Meanwhile, oil spread throughout a ruptured tank through the port side blister and into the lower parts of the ship. Negeshi and Kaido had just knocked *California* out of the war for the next two and a half years.

By now, the *Akagi*'s torpedoes had turned battleship row into a disaster area. The *West Virginia* looked ready to capsize, and the *Oklahoma* was about to turn turtle. Around the capital ships, the harbor water turned obsidian as fuel oil spewed from their shattered tanks. The oil would soon ignite, transforming the scene into a hellish nightmare of thick smoke and flames.

But for all the damage inflicted at this point, the American gunners stayed at their stations and began to find the range just as the *Akagi*'s final group of three Kates began their runs, joined by the two strays from *Hiryu*. The final three went after the crippled *Oklahoma*, while one of the *Hiryu*'s pilots delivered another fish into the *West Virginia*. Matsumura was the other stray from the *Hiryu*'s group and, as he tried to line up on the *Oklahoma*, he got caught in the prop wash from the plane in front of him. It bounced him around so violently, that he broke off the attack and made a 360-degree turn under fire to start another run, just as the *Kaga*'s Kates joined the fight.

After the last of the *Akagi*'s B5Ns cleared the area, the *Soryu*'s lone wolf, Juzo Mori, made his attack on the *California*, probably scoring a hit on her that condemned her to a slow, steady descent to the harbor bottom.

Though hit hard, the American defenders manned their anti-aircraft guns with a professionalism that thoroughly impressed the Japanese. Even the first wave of Kates had encountered some flak, but by the end of the attack, the entire harbor was alive with muzzle flashes. Into this maelstrom, the *Kaga*'s Kates went, and they were swatted out of the sky.

The first string of three struggled through the counter-fire to attack the *West Virginia*. Two of them were hit before completing their runs. Slightly behind and to the left, the next string of three angled for the *Oklahoma*. The lead plane in this string, flown by Petty Officer 1st Class Shigeo Sato, was hit eight times but was able to release on the dying battleship, inflicting further misery on the *Oklahoma*'s crew. His number two wingman was badly hit, and his gunner was critically wounded. The third Kate did not survive. Flown by Airman 1st Class Syuzo Kitahara,

the torpedo bomber took a direct hit in the fuel line and burst into flames. As the aircraft streaked across the sky with a thick tail of fire, Kitahara's gunner jumped from the cockpit. He landed near the *California*, where he died a few minutes later. The B5N continued on to crash near the hospital, where a marine on the scene snagged one of Kitahara's boots as a souvenir from the pilot's dismembered remains.

Much worse awaited the final six torpedo bombers of the attack. As they narrowed the range to battleship row, the Americans threw up a veritable wall of anti-aircraft and machine-gun fire. One shell detonated the flight leader's torpedo and his Kate blew apart in midair right over the submarine base. The engine was blasted clear, while the rest of the wreck came down and was later recovered.

The second Kate pilot evaded the anti-aircraft fire and dropped another torpedo on the *West Virginia*. His wingman, the last plane in this stream, targeted the *Nevada*. This was Petty Officer 2nd Class Kenichi Kumamoto. He stayed on his attack run, even as American counter-fire stitched his plane. Just after he released his torpedo, Kumamoto's Kate exploded in flames and crashed just aft of his battleship target. His torpedo scored a direct hit, tearing a hole 48 feet long and 25 feet wide some 14 feet above the keel. The damage proved so severe that *Nevada*'s crew had to counter flood. She continued to take on water for a month after the attack as a result of Kumamoto's torpedo.

As Kumamoto cleared the area, the final six *Kaga* Kates hugged the deck, passed over the submarine base, and flew into the hailstorm of anti-aircraft fire. The flight leader, Hirotokae Iwata somehow slipped through to score the last hit of the attack. His torpedo churned through the oil-covered harbor water, reached *Oklahoma*, and went through one of the holes torn in the hull by another torpedo. As *Oklahoma* rolled over, she shuddered as this weapon detonated deep inside her bowels, a devastating coup de grace.

Behind Iwata, his section was wiped out. American gunners clawed down his number two, and even 60 years later his plane has not been recovered from the Southeast Loch. The third Kate in the string also took devastating hits. The pilot jettisoned his torpedo, which landed on the dock next to USS *Barley*. The plane limped to Fort Weaver, where it subsequently crashed.

Five of the 12 *Kaga* Kates had been shot down. Their attack demonstrated how vulnerable the B5N could be to alert American anti-aircraft gunners and would serve as a harbinger for things to come.

By 0815, the torpedo attack on Pearl Harbor had come to an end. For a loss of slightly over 10 percent of the strike force, the Japanese crews had scored big. The *Akagi*'s pilots sank *Oklahoma* and *West Virginia* with their outstanding attack. Strays from the *Soryu* and *Hiryu*, as well as some of the *Kaga*'s aircraft, hit both ships even as they sank, contributing to the damage the Americans would need to repair in the coming months. Altogether, those two battleships absorbed between 14 and 19 torpedo hits, almost half of the total number the Japanese carried into the attack that morning. Had the Japanese possessed better plane-to-plane communications, they might have used those later torpedoes against the *California* or *Nevada* where they would have been more usefully employed.

As it was, a few bold pilots chose the *California* and *Nevada* as their targets. Three selected the *California*, and their torpedoes did enough damage to cause the *California* to sink over the ensuing days. The hit the doomed Kumamoto scored on the *Nevada* crippled the ship and helped ensure she would remain out of the war for months to come. These three brave crews contributed more than most to extending the carnage along battleship row.

While the *Akagi*'s torpedo squadron shined that morning in the harbor, the planes from the *Hiryu* and *Soryu* had much less success. Sixteen of their planes loosed 15 of their torpedoes against ancillary targets at best. Only five dropped on their primary objectives: the American capital ships. After the war, several of the pilots from these two squadrons wrote scathing analyses of their performance. Nakajima was particularly hard on himself when he wrote in 1951, "During the training period, identification of ships was stressed, but I failed in a time of real fighting."

The *Kaga*'s squadron, even as it lost almost half its planes, achieved little more. As American anti-aircraft fire shredded their ranks, they were able to score only one significant hit, Kumamoto's strike on the *Nevada*. Their other torpedoes, directed at the *Oklahoma* and *West Virginia*, served only to increase the damage done to these already doomed ships.

Taken by one of Mitsuo Fuchida's high-level Kate bombers, this remarkable combat photograph shows the damage wrought primarily by the *Akagi* and *Kaga*'s Kate crews. At right, USS *West Virginia* has already suffered catastrophic damage and is listing hard to port. Only quick counter-flooding saved her from turning turtle. Behind her, the *Oklahoma*'s shattered hull is bleeding oil as she begins to capsize. *Vestal* and *Arizona* appear to be relatively undamaged in this photograph, which historian David Aiken contends is evidence that the doomed battleship was not struck by a torpedo in the moments before the level bombers achieved her complete destruction.

For all the mistakes caused by the "friction of war," the 40 Kate crews carried out their mission and succeeded in sinking the *West Virginia*, *Oklahoma*, *California*, *Oglala*, and *Utah*. Their weapons also crippled the *Nevada* and the *Raleigh* and seriously damaged the *Helena*. It was a remarkable achievement, and it was these crews who caused the most grievous harm to the American Pacific Fleet that morning. While Fuchida's high-level bombers destroyed the *Arizona*, many of their modified naval gun shells-turned-bombs failed to detonate properly and did not inflict substantial harm on the other ships moored by Ford Island that day.

The first blows had been struck. Now it remained to be seen if the Japanese could follow up their success at Pearl Harbor and destroy the remaining capital ships of the U.S. Pacific Fleet. In the months to come, the same crews who devastated Pearl Harbor would get that chance four times over.

Part I

1942: INITIATIVE

THE JAPANESE CAPTURED THE INITIATIVE IN THE PACIFIC WITH THEIR DARING PEARL HARBOR ATTACK AND SPENT THE NEXT YEAR TRYING DESPERATELY TO RETAIN IT. In 1942, the Japanese and Americans were almost evenly matched for the only time in the Pacific War. They possessed a roughly even number of carriers and aircraft in the theater. Both sides risked their carrier assets in a series of bruising battles where the strategic initiative hinged on the outcome. In the end, the Japanese sacrificed the bulk of their carrier-based airpower by the fall of 1942 and lost the initiative anyway. It was perhaps one of the best displays of American strategic acumen in that country's history. But it came at a cost. By the end of the year, the U.S. Navy had only one fully operational fleet carrier left in the Pacific, the USS *Enterprise*.

(opposite) The U.S. Navy started the war with the Douglas TBD Devastator as its primary torpedo bomber. Slow, non-maneuverable, and under-armed, it was cold meat for attacking Zeroes. This TBD belonged to VT-6 off the *Enterprise*. After Midway, where three TBD squadrons were wiped out, the surviving TBDs were withdrawn from the fleet and replaced by the TBF Avenger.

念記業卒　其飛行練習生

Japan's secret weapon against the U.S. fleet was its prewar aviation cadet classes. Trained to a razor's edge, tempered in battle over China, these pilots and their crews had no peer in 1942. In fact, they were probably some of the best combat aviators of the 20th century. By the end of 1942, most were dead, killed in the furious battles at Coral Sea, Midway, and off Guadalcanal. Almost 90 percent of these men failed to survive the war.

Land-based aviation units played little role in anti-ship missions in 1942. Inaccurate bombing techniques, inadequate numbers, and misguided prewar doctrine hampered the U.S. Army Air Force and ensured that its brave crews would fail repeatedly to stop Japanese convoys and invasion fleets. For the Japanese, their Army Air Force took part in almost no anti-shipping operations, while the Imperial Japanese Navy's (IJN) land-based G3M and G4M bomber squadrons sustained heavy losses every time they went up against the U.S. Navy.

Three pivotal battles wrested the strategic initiative away from the Japanese: Coral Sea, Midway, and the campaign at Guadalcanal. By year's end, Japan had been forced back irrevocably on the defensive, the heart of its navy torn away in a year's bitter fighting.

(above) The U.S. Navy's 1942 air groups contained three different types of aircraft with vastly different ranges, altitude capabilities, and cruising speeds. This made launching coordinated full air group strikes extremely difficult. The TBD in particular caused many problems since it could not keep up with the other aircraft when laden with a torpedo. The air groups tinkered with the prewar launch doctrines hoping to find a way around the problem, but it was never really solved until the arrival of the F6F and TBF later in the war.

(right) For the U.S. Army Air Force, anti-shipping missions in 1942 accomplished little. Chained to a prewar doctrine of high-altitude precision bombing, the army air force sent its B-17 Flying Fortresses against many Japanese task forces with very little results. Prior to the war, the U.S. Army Air Force had justified the expense of the big Boeing bomber by claiming it could defend America's shores through long-range, high-altitude attacks. As a result, President Roosevelt dispatched the 19th Bomb Group and other B-17 reinforcements to the Philippines shortly before Pearl Harbor in the hopes that the Forts could stop any Japanese amphibious invasion headed for the islands. The doctrine turned out to be a complete failure, as free-falling bombs from 20,000 feet or higher stood almost no chance of hitting a maneuvering ship.

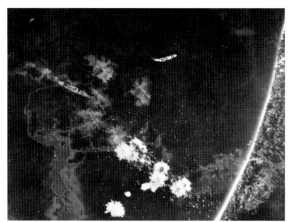

(above and above right) The U.S. Army Air Force tries to destroy shipping in the early part of the war. These high-level attacks rarely did any damage, though the Fortress crews almost always reported vast numbers of ships sunk or crippled. From 20,000 feet, the smoke from anti-aircraft fire and their own bombs exploding on the water made their attacks look quite impressive and successful. The reality was that as an anti-shipping weapon, the B-17 was a failure. Consequently, the U.S. Army Air Force inflicted very little damage on the Japanese Navy in 1942. This particular raid took place in November 1942 against a Japanese landing force at Tonelei Harbor in the northern Solomons.

(right center) In August, the U.S. 1st Marine Division captured this unfinished airfield from the Japanese at Guadalcanal in the southern Solomons. The offensive caught the Japanese totally by surprise, and through the fall the Imperial Navy and Army sought to recapture the airstrip. As the campaign unfolded, the American planes based at Henderson Field controlled the seaward approaches to Guadalcanal. Each Japanese attempt to reinforce its troops on the island met with heavy losses from air attack.

(right) The American carrier Enterprise takes a bomb hit during the Battle of Eastern Solomons. Though battered, the Enterprise survived to see more action than any other American fleet carrier in history.

(above) The anti-aircraft cruiser USS *Atlanta* steams with four destroyers. The *Atlanta* and her sister ships formed the backbone of the carrier task force's escort screen in the second half of 1942. At Santa Cruz, they threw up a tremendous volume of fire that savaged the incoming Japanese air strikes. Unfortunately, both the *Atlanta* and *Juneau* were thrown away during night surface engagements off Guadalcanal, a role for which they were ill-suited.

(left) The Mitsubishi G4M "Betty" bomber formed the backbone of Japan's long-range shored-based anti-shipping capabilities. At the outset of the war, G4M crews had helped sink the British battleship *Prince of Wales* and the battle cruiser *Repulse*. Despite that success, when facing modern fleet air defenses, the Betty units took tremendous losses due to their light construction and propensity to catch fire when hit.

Chapter Two

Hammer and Anvil: Death Ride of the Carrier *Shoho*

ON MAY 7, 1942, MEDAL OF HONOR RECIPIENT ADMIRAL FRANK "BLACK JACK" FLETCHER STOOD IN THE *YORKTOWN'S* FLAG PLOT ONE DECK BELOW THE NAVIGATION BRIDGE AND CONSIDERED THE MESSAGE HE'D JUST RECEIVED. Two hours before, at 0600 hours, the *Yorktown* had launched 10 Scouting Five SBD Dauntless dive bombers. They fanned out into a northwest-to-northeast search pattern with orders to hunt for Japanese ships out to 250 miles. Fletcher knew, thanks to the code-breaking efforts of U.S. Naval Intelligence, that the Japanese were heading for him with at least two fleet carriers. He just didn't know where they were, and for the last five days he'd shadowboxed with a confusing array of Imperial Navy task forces. That day, in the Coral Sea, everyone sensed a coming fight.

The message he received proved to be the catalyst. One of the SBD scouts reported sighting two Japanese carriers and four cruisers about 175 miles northwest of Fletcher's ships. That sealed it—the *Shokaku* and *Zuikaku*, veterans of the Pearl Harbor raid, had been found.

(opposite) Admiral Frank "Black Jack" Fletcher, maligned by most postwar historians for his conduct during the Guadalcanal campaign, took a great risk at Coral Sea, launching all his aircraft against a single contact report on May 7, 1942.

Fletcher, a balding, severe-looking traditionalist who had just celebrated his 57th birthday a week before, was not a naval aviator. Graduating in the top third of his academy class in 1906, he'd spent his life in the black shoe navy. A courageous man personally, on this morning, based on this sole report, he took an enormous gamble.

Prewar exercises had shown the navy that a carrier-to-carrier battle would probably occur at some point in a war against Japan. Exactly how to fight such an unusual battle with no precedent preoccupied the carrier commanders through much of the interwar years. One conclusion emerged from all the war games and exercises: the flat-top that struck first almost always won the battle.

For this reason, Fletcher didn't hesitate. He ordered a full strike against the distant Japanese force. His own ships would have to ride out any Japanese counterattack with minimal air cover. Only about 20 F4F Wildcats would remain behind to fly patrol over the American ships.

Fletcher had two carriers in the Coral Sea that morning. Admiral Aubrey Fitch, in tactical control of the battle, raised his flag on the USS *Lexington*. Together with the *Yorktown*, the Americans would be able to fling almost 100 planes against the Japanese carriers.

The *Lexington* launched its air group first. Air Group Two's air group commander (CAG), Bill Ault, wanted his four squadrons to form up and head for the Japanese ships as a cohesive force. His squadrons put up 25 SBD Dauntless dive bombers, 12 Douglas TBD Devastators, and 10 Grumman F4F Wildcats. They circled around the *Lexington* until all the aircraft had found their slots in each squadron formation before finally heading out to the Japanese task force.

Meanwhile, the *Yorktown* delayed her launch for about 20 minutes. Instead of organizing over the carrier, the air group commander, Oscar Pederson, decided to send his torpedo squadron out on its own while the SBDs and F4Fs formed up together. Then, the dive bombers and fighters would catch up to the Devastators en route to the target area. The *Yorktown* launched 25 SBDs from VS-5 and VB-5, followed by the TBDs of VT-5. Fighting Forty-Two's Wildcats rolled down the deck last, getting airborne just as the last of the Devastators disappeared to the north.

By mid-morning, 93 American aircraft filled the sky over the Coral Sea. It was the largest strike force the U.S. Navy assembled for one attack until the Rabaul raids in November 1943.

Scouting SBD Dauntless dive bombers return to the *Yorktown*. A transmission error resulted in one SBD crew sending a false contact report that Fletcher immediately acted upon. After the crew returned to the *Yorktown* and explained they had not seen any Japanese carriers but had meant to report two cruisers instead, Fletcher lost his temper and berated the aviators, thinking that he'd just committed two air groups to an ancillary target at best.

With her deck clear, the *Yorktown* recovered her scouts. The pilot who radioed the contact report was brought before Fletcher. Here, the young naval aviator tried to explain that he and his back seater had made a coding error. Instead of sighting two carriers and four cruisers, he had seen two cruisers and four destroyers—a minor force at best. He'd attempted to correct the mistake, but he had lost contact with the *Yorktown* and was unable to radio a new report.

Ninety-three planes heading in the wrong direction—the reality of the error sent Fletcher into a fury. He tongue-lashed the shaken junior officer and finished by shouting, "You've just cost the United States two carriers!"

The *Shoho* takes its first hits. Smoke streams off the flight deck as she remains steady into the wind even as either a near miss or a torpedo hit strikes her starboard side.

With their decks empty and no reserves below decks, the two American carriers had shot their bolt. Should the Japanese sight the *Yorktown* or *Lexington*, a catastrophe would follow and Fletcher's near-defenseless force would be crushed.

But the Japanese were not at the top of their game either that morning. Their scouts found Fletcher's refueling force, the oiler *Neosho* and her escorting tin can, USS *Sims*. The Japanese scout sent a contact report announcing it had found an American carrier. To Fletcher's southeast, the *Zuikaku* and *Shokaku*—the two fleet carriers Fletcher thought he was attacking—promptly launched 76 planes. Ironically, the Japanese shot their bolt at a minor target as well.

As Fletcher considered recalling his aircraft, another contact report arrived. An army air force bomber had spotted a Japanese carrier only 30 miles from the original SBD contact report. Rather than aborting the strike, the *Yorktown* sent a message giving the coordinates of the new target to attack. Fletcher could only hope there really was an aircraft carrier there this time.

In fact, the U.S. Army Air Force report was accurate. The American crew had spotted the light carrier *Shoho*, which, along with her screen, had been tasked to provide cover for the amphibious assault force bound for Port Moresby.

Shortly before 1100 hours, Lieutenant Commander Weldon Hamilton spotted the Japanese ships far to his north. The sky was crystal clear that morning, and visibility extended for miles in all directions. Through his binoculars, he picked up a series of wakes that could only be a task force.

Bill Ault brought his air group around in a starboard turn to the right. Only a few minutes later, they could make out the Japanese ships. They'd found the *Shoho* loosely covered by four cruisers and a destroyer. Ault ordered a coordinated attack—he would follow the navy's prewar attack doctrine closely on this day.

The Oregonian and his two wingmen dove on the carrier first. Meanwhile, his scouting squadron, VS-2, under Lieutenant Commander Robert E. Dixon, looped around to the north to get up sun.

Ault's three charging SBDs prompted a quick reaction from the carrier, which began a radical turn to port. The sudden move caused all three pilots to miss their target, though one bomb landed close enough to blow several planes off the carrier's deck.

The turn also screwed up Scouting Two. Instead of attacking lengthwise down the deck of the flat-top, Dixon's men suddenly found themselves making a beam attack

(above) A torpedo explodes amidships on the Shoho's starboard side, throwing up a tremendous geyser of water and smoke over the flight deck.

(right) The Lexington's Devastators pile in on the Shoho. Torpedo hits have kicked up huge roiling clouds of smoke over the Shoho as two TBDs come off target.

(below right) The Shoho during Air Group 5's attack, a few minutes after Bill Ault led Air Group 2 back toward the Lady Lex. The flight deck burns furiously, probably as a result of Bill Burch and Swede Vejtasa's hits. This photograph quite possibly could have been taken from Vejtasa's SBD by the Yorktown's gunner officer, who flew in the SBD's rear seat that day.

with a crosswind to boot. To his extreme disappointment, all his pilots missed, their bombs blasting water spouts all around their target.

At this point, the *Shoho*'s skipper, Captain Ishonosuke Izawa, made a critical error. With the SBDs of Scouting Two now finished with their dive-bombing runs, a slight lull developed. Doctrine demanded that the bombing and torpedo squadrons go in together after the scouting squadron had suppressed the enemy task force. Hamilton's VB-2 had been forced to wait for Torpedo Two's ponderously slow Devastators, which were closing on the *Shoho* from the southwest.

Thinking he had enough time to launch more fighters from his deck, Izawa ordered the *Shoho* into the wind. Just as she steadied on a southeasterly course, Torpedo Two's TBDs began streaming around the *Shoho*'s escorting cruisers. They penetrated the screen with ease and then split to launch an anvil attack. Half the squadron would strike from the port bow, half from the starboard. Prewar tests had shown this to be the most effective way of striking a moving ship.

Hamilton went in at the same time. With the *Shoho* committed to launching her ready fighters, she could not evade either attack. Though three planes managed to get off her deck, Hamilton scored a direct hit just forward of her aft elevator with a 1,000-pound bomb. Seconds later, one of his other pilots planted his thousand-pounder right behind the forward elevator.

By now, Torpedo Two's TBDs had swung into their final runs on both sides of the *Shoho*. Led by Lieutenant Commander Leonard Thornhill, the Devastators executed a near-perfect attack. Thornhill's torpedo struck home first, gouging the *Shoho*'s hull on the starboard quarter. The blast wrecked the *Shoho*'s steering gear, ensuring she would not be able to evade any of the subsequent attacks. Unable to alter course, she took four more torpedo hits from VT-2's 12 aircraft. Almost

half of their weapons had struck home. It was to be one of the best torpedo attacks executed by any U.S. Navy squadron during World War II.

Crippled, the *Shoho* staggered onward even as the *Yorktown*'s air group arrived. The dive bombers from Scouting and Bombing Five hit the light carrier no fewer than 11 times. As the SBDs pounded the flat-top, VT-5's Devastators scored two more torpedo hits. Captain Izawa ordered his crew to abandon ship. Four minutes later, the *Shoho*'s shattered hull plunged beneath the waves. Less than half her crew survived.

The destruction of the *Shoho* ranks as the single most successful combined attack the navy launched using its prewar doctrine. In the weeks and months to come, the flaws of the prewar theorists would be revealed and new methods of attack, along with new and more capable aircraft, would be developed. Yet, at this one moment early in the Pacific War, everything went the U.S. Navy's way, and the Japanese lost their first of 20 aircraft carriers that would be sunk over the next three years.

As for Fletcher, no Japanese bombs rained down on his carriers that morning. Instead, the Japanese sank the *Sims* and *Neosho*. The Americans had won the first round, but the main event remained to be fought.

Air Group 5's SBDs head for home, their work done for the day. This extremely rare aerial photograph was actually taken three days earlier when the *Yorktown*'s planes attacked a Japanese landing force at Tulagi Harbor in the Solomons.

Chapter Three

Carrier against Carrier

AFTER THE EVENTS OF MAY 7, FLETCHER WASN'T GOING TO TAKE ANY CHANCES WITH THE NEXT MORNING'S SEARCH. INSTEAD OF THE 10 SBDS LAUNCHED THE MORNING BEFORE, THE *LEXINGTON* USED 18 OF ITS REMAINING DAUNTLESS DIVE BOMBERS FOR AN AROUND-THE-COMPASS SEARCH EMPHASIZING THE NORTH. It paid off. Shortly after 0800, one of the *Lexington's* scouts located the elusive *Shokaku* and *Zuikaku* through a gap in the overcast north of the American task force.

The *Yorktown* and *Lexington* launched everything they had left—some 75 planes. Once again, Bill Ault had his Air Group Two form up over the *Lexington*, while the *Yorktown's* planes assembled en route, thus saving fuel. On the way to their targets, bad weather hampered both air groups. Rain squalls and scattered, thick clouds blotted out the view of the ocean below and forced a number of planes from the *Lexington* to abort altogether.

(opposite) Cleaning the rear seat gunner's weapons on an SBD prior to launch. The Dauntless dive bombers usually carried either a pair of .30-caliber machine guns or a single .50 in the rear cockpit. Against the Japanese Zeroes' determined interception, the guns offered minimal defensive protection.

(right) A Dauntless taxis to its launch position, toting a 500-pound bomb. The SBD proved to be very stable in a steep dive, thanks in part to its large, perforated dive flaps, which are under the wings.

The *Yorktown*'s Dauntless dive bombers
hammer away at the *Shokaku*. Two near
misses have sprouted on the carrier's
starboard side.

The *Yorktown*'s senior strike pilots confer prior to the mission against the
Shokaku and *Zuikaku*. At left is VT-5's skipper, Lieutenant Commander Joe
Taylor. Scouting Five's leader, Lieutenant Commander Bill Burch, is standing
beside Taylor at right. Burch scored a direct hit on the *Shoho* on May 7. The
following day, he led the *Yorktown*'s dive bombers against the *Shokaku*.

An excellent study of the telescopic scope the SBD pilots at Coral Sea used.
Sudden changes in altitude and humidity levels caused the scope and the
Dauntless' windscreen to fog. This problem led to many misses in combat at
Coral Sea and was not properly fixed until the summer and early fall of 1942.

The *Shokaku* runs hard a few seconds after the last photo was taken. Air Group 5 scored two hits on the carrier, temporarily knocking its flight deck out of action. A short time later, Bill Ault, AG-2's commander, scored the final hit that knocked the *Shokaku* out of the battle.

At 1032, despite the weather, the *Yorktown*'s dive bombers found the Japanese carriers. Led by Scouting Five's Bill Burch, the Dauntless dive bombers had reached the area before the slower Devastators. Rather than initiating an immediate attack, Burch adhered to prewar doctrine and waited for the TBDs so they could all go in together. It was a mistake that perhaps cost the Americans the chance to sink a major Japanese fleet asset.

As Burch's planes circled among the clouds south of their targets, the Japanese remained unaware of their presence. The combat air patrol was thin, and the opportunity to strike was perfect. Yet Burch continued to wait until the TBD's finally arrived. But by then, the ships below had awakened to the danger, and the carriers scrambled their ready fighters.

Burch led the VS-5s down in a 70-degree screaming dive against the *Shokaku*. The steep dive through the humid South Pacific skies, though, caused their windscreens to fog. Unable to see well, all the scout pilots missed the flat-top.

Moments later, Lieutenant Wally Short led his 17 VB-5 SBDs down after circling around to set up a better attack. As they entered their dives, the Zero CAP intercepted them. The Mitsubishis crippled Lieutenant John Powers' SBD, setting it afire. Nevertheless, Powers stayed in his dive. A thousand feet above the *Shokaku*, he dropped his bomb, which struck the fleet carrier next to the island, sending up a sheet of smoke and flame. It was the last act of a very courageous man. Powers' Dauntless exploded a split-second later and crashed into the sea next to his stricken target. For his selfless role in crippling the *Shokaku*, Powers received a posthumous Medal of Honor.

One other *Yorktown* SBD planted a bomb on the *Shokaku*. Hit twice with her flight deck temporarily out of commission, the *Shokaku* had been badly damaged.

Torpedo Five showed up during the dive-bombing attack, hoping to deliver the coup de grace. Instead, the TBD crews faced a firestorm of anti-aircraft fire. The flak proved so thick that the pilots could not press their attacks. Releasing at maximum range, none of the torpedoes hit home.

Everything now depended on the *Lexington*'s Air Group Two.

Struggling through the overcast, Bill Ault's squadrons became scattered. When Ault reached the last known position of the Japanese force, he found only cloudy skies and empty ocean. He and the rest of his men had missed an updated contact report broadcast by their ship. Undeterred, Ault began a box-pattern search which quickly yielded results. While flying north, the Americans spotted the Japanese carriers 15 miles to the west of their port wings. Ault began to orbit, calling for VB-2 and its 11 SDBs. Try as he might, he could not raise them. Bombing Two had run low on fuel and was forced to abort.

A TBD Devastator returns home. Though the TBDs inflicted tremendous damage on the *Shoho* the day before, against the *Shokaku* neither of the two torpedo squadrons managed a hit. The *Shokaku* maneuvered expertly throughout the attacks, and the air defenses protecting the two Japanese fleet carriers were much more lethal than what the Americans had experienced over the *Shoho*.

Ault's four SBDs and the TBDs of VT-2 were all that the Americans had left. The Oregonian brought them in.

Once again, the *Shokaku* fought back fiercely. Zeroes disrupted the attackers, but Ault pushed over and drove hard for the flat-top in a 70-degree descent. At the last possible second, he toggled his bomb, which plummeted down into the *Shokaku*, exploding on the starboard side of the flight deck. This hit effectively knocked the *Shokaku* out of the battle. She was out of action until August.

As Ault's four SBDs made their runs, the *Lexington*'s TBD's came down from 6,000 feet and tried to hit *Shokaku*'s starboard side. Like the *Yorktown*'s torpedo planes, though, they faced heavy anti-aircraft fire and scored no hits.

Bill Ault was never seen again after his attack. Chased by Zeroes, badly damaged, he became lost in the overcast. Though the *Lexington* picked up some of his radio transmissions, his aircraft vanished into the Coral Sea. The navy had lost one of its great early fighting leaders of the air.

The Americans had had their chance. They'd knocked the *Shokaku* out of the battle, but had not delivered any fatal blows. Now, the Japanese would have their turn.

As the Americans hit the Japanese flat-tops, the *Zuikaku*'s and *Shokaku*'s air groups overwhelmed the air defenses protecting the *Lexington* and *Yorktown*. The Wildcat CAP tried its best to drive the attackers off, but sheer numbers swamped them.

In a masterful coordinated strike, the Japanese hammered the *Lexington* with two torpedo and two bomb hits. The huge battle-cruiser-turned-carrier at first appeared to weather the damage, though a ruptured fuel tank spread deadly fumes throughout the ship. That afternoon, a spark in a generator room touched off the gas and consumed the *Lady Lex* in a gigantic explosion. Subsequent secondary blasts doomed the ship, and at 1607 her crew streamed over the side and into the water. She sank at 2000.

The same attack that morning also hit the *Yorktown*. A 250-kilogram bomb penetrated the flight deck and exploded deep inside the ship, causing many casualties. The damage did not prevent flight operations, and the *Yorktown* recovered her strike and as many aircraft from the *Lexington* as she could handle before turning south and running for home.

The peculiar battle of Coral Sea came to an end that afternoon with both sides retiring. Though the Japanese scored a tactical victory—the first of many against the U.S. Navy in 1942, they failed to take Port Moresby, a terrible strategic failure. Moreover, both the *Shokaku*'s and *Zuikaku*'s air groups had been hit hard and would need time to be rebuilt and retrained. With the *Shokaku* damaged and over 200 of her crew killed or wounded, she would be out of action for the next four months. Perhaps the greatest effect Coral Sea had on the course of the Pacific War was the absence of the *Shokaku* and *Zuikaku* at Midway. Had they been in shape to join the Kido Butai in June, the battle of Midway quite probably would have ended in a Japanese victory.

(above) During the Japanese attack, the *Lexington* took two bombs and two torpedo hits. Originally laid down as a battle cruiser, the *Lexington* was not nearly as agile as the *Yorktown* and had a very difficult time evading torpedoes. The Japanese hit her with an anvil attack, and her skipper maneuvered against both without committing to turning fully into either of them. The results were two hits on the starboard side. The *Lady Lex* smokes after the attack as Dauntless dive bombers and an F4F with its gear down pass overhead.

(right) The *Lexington*'s debris-strewn flight deck after the attack.

(top) Despite her damage, the *Lexington* was able to resume flight operations and take her aircraft aboard after the Japanese strike had departed. In the foreground, is the destruction wrought on one of the anti-aircraft gun galleries.

(above) Rocked by internal explosions caused by a ruptured fuel tank, the *Lexington* suffered catastrophic damage later that afternoon, forcing the crew to abandon ship. She's wreathed in smoke and flames.

(above) The end of a *Shokaku* B5N Kate. Damaged during the attack by anti-aircraft fire, it crash landed on Indispensable Reef en route home. It was found and photographed by the U.S. Navy after the battle had ended.

(left) The *Lexington*'s final moments.

Chapter Four

The Birth of "Joint Attack"

AT 0540 HOURS ON JUNE 4, 1942, MARINE SCOUT BOMBING SQUADRON 241 WAS READY FOR THE DAY. Already in the cockpits of their SBD Dauntless dive bombers and Chance-Vought SB2U Vindicator dive bombers, everyone in the squadron knew that today they would be facing the mighty Combined Fleet. Just before dawn, they had assembled on the flight line to warm their engines and wait for word to head out against the Japanese fleet.

In fact, all up and down the flight line, Midway's aerial defenders ran their engines so they'd be ready in case the word to scramble came through.

Ten minutes later, the Vindicator pilots got word to shut down their engines. This puzzled Captain Bruce Prosser and some of the pilots, since just as they complied with the new order the fighters of VMF-221 taxied out to the runway and took off. Nearby, the Grumman TBF-1 Avengers of Torpedo Eight's Midway detachment also began to roll. Something was up.

(opposite) The American airfield at Midway Atoll.

(right) Torpedo Eight received the first production batch of TBF-1 Avengers in the spring of 1942. While the rest of the squadron embarked on the USS *Hornet*, the six TBFs that had joined VT-8 were detached and sent to Pearl Harbor. From there, they flew to Midway and operated as an independent element until virtually wiped out on the morning of June 4, 1942. This photograph shows 8-T-1 at Norfolk in April, shortly before Lieutenant Langdon Fieberling led his small band west. Bert Earnest, Jay Manning, and Harry Ferrier took 8-T-1 into battle at Midway two months later.

At least the navy pilots had some information. Just before 0600, a jeep drove up to Lieutenant Langdon Fieberling's Avenger. A captain jumped out to tell him the Japanese fleet was 150 miles out to the northwest. Fieberling, who was Torpedo Eight's detachment commander, pulled himself out of the cockpit and, from the wing, began shouting to his other pilots, "Steer 320, 150 miles out!" Mechanics rushed from plane to plane passing the word to make sure everyone had heard it. That was it—the full extent of their briefing for a mission against the most heavily defended fleet in the world.

Just after 0600, their six Avengers broke free of the runway and disappeared to the northwest.

Watching all this left Prosser puzzled. What was going on? They'd just cut their engines, but now it looked as if Midway was launching a strike.

The B-26 Marauders went next. These Army Air Force bombers had flown in only a short time before as a last-minute reinforcement for the Midway garrison. The four planes, under the command of Captain James Collins, each carried a single torpedo under the fuselage. This was a unique situation for the crews, since none had ever dropped a torpedo and had received only a few vague oral instructions on how to do it. Only a week before, they'd been scheduled to leave Hawaii to join the 22nd and 38th Bomb Groups in Australia. None of the crews had ever even practiced an anti-shipping attack.

Nonetheless, they too rumbled off into the early morning sky over Midway, following the TBFs as they disappeared over the horizon.

At this point, Prosser and the other marines decided they couldn't delay their takeoff any longer. They gunned their engines and headed out to the runway. It was now well after 0600.

Most of the men in VMSB-241 had very little time in Dauntless dive bombers, but some of the pilots, including 2nd Lieutenant Sumner Whitten, had plenty of experience in SB2Us. Unfortunately, none of the leaders had much tactical training, and they had decided in the days before the battle began to use a glide bombing attack instead of a dive-bombing one. Glide bombing was easier to execute for inexperienced pilots, but it also made them more vulnerable to flak and fighters.

A few days before, the army, navy, and marine detachment and squadron leaders had met to hash out how they would attack the Japanese. The plan they devised envisioned a combined attack covered by VMF-221's fighters. The torpedo planes—the navy Avengers and army Marauders—would link up and orbit after takeoff, waiting for the marines to get airborne. Then, they'd all go in together and hit the Japanese simultaneously.

It didn't work out that way. For the marines, takeoff from Midway became a scene of complete confusion. Vindicators and Dauntless dive bombers staggered into the air, laden with fuel and ordnance. Among the last planes off from Midway that morning was Sumner Whitten's SB2U. As he departed, the Japanese 108-plane strike arrived and began pitching bombs around the runway. Another minute or so, and the last planes from VMSB-241 would have been shot down as they took off.

Somehow, the 12 Vindicators untangled themselves from the SBDs and formed up into one group. Major Lofton Henderson, the squadron commander, took the 16 SBDs and led them off in a second group. They were supposed to stay together, but the SBDs cruised much faster than the old "Wind Indicators" and the two groups soon drifted apart.

Not long after forming up, something inside Bruce Prosser's engine exploded. A chunk of the cowl blew off and fluttered away into the slipstream. He reversed course and limped back to Midway, done for the morning. That left the squadron executive officer, Major Ben Norris, with 11 SB2Us to lead against the Japanese fleet.

The torpedo bombers were nowhere to be seen. In fact, rather than wait for everyone else, Fieberling simply pointed his nose at the Japanese fleet and headed out. A few miles behind them, Collins' Marauders did the same thing—so much for a combined attack.

And the fact that VMF-221 had launched to intercept the incoming Japanese raid ensured the bombers would not receive any escort that morning. Piecemeal, they flew into the heart of Japan's strategic naval power, the four fleet carriers of the Kido Butai.

Around 0700, the TBFs found the Japanese carrier force. At 4,000 feet, they could see the Kido Butai stretched across the horizon in front of them. They began to let down to attack altitude when the Japanese CAP struck.

About 30 Zeroes sallied to the defense of their flight decks. Within seconds, the Avengers were swamped by fighters attacking from all directions. The gunners poured fire in return, and several A6Ms were hit or shot down. But without fighter escort, without a combined attack, the men of Torpedo Eight stood no chance.

(above) A torpedo-armed Martin B-26 Marauder. In order to carry the heavy anti-ship weapon, the B-26s were modified and the torpedo was slung under the belly on an external rack. At Midway, the crews had no time to learn how to accurately drop a torpedo from their speeding bombers.

(left) The Chance-Vought SB2U Vindicator made history as the first monoplane carrier-based dive-bomber the U.S. Navy acquired. By 1942, however, it was hopelessly obsolete.

Inside 8-T-1, Ensign Bert Earnest dipped his nose and picked up speed as he made his diving approach to attack position. Behind him, his teenage gunners Jay Manning and Harry Ferrier frantically tried to defend their aircraft. Manning, a native of Washington, was swinging his turret, tracking and shooting at the careening Zeroes. Nearby, one Avenger after another erupted in flames and plunged into the water. In the TBFs belly, 17-year-old Harry Ferrier peered out one of the side windows in time to see Ensign Charles Brannon's TBF mushroom into a ball of fire. Stunned by the sight, he turned and manned his .30-caliber peashooter in the bottom of the fuselage.

Above him, he heard a sudden thump and Manning's gun went silent. The Washingtonian had taken a 20-millimeter round right in the chest, killing him instantly and sending a spray of blood cascading down the sides of the fuselage.

The Avenger lurched as more cannon and machine-gun rounds hit home. The hydraulics failed, causing the tail wheel to drop down right in front of Harry Ferrier's .30-caliber gun. With no clear field of fire, he was helpless to defend 8-T-1. Seconds later, a machine-gun round pierced the fuselage and shot off Harry's wrist watch. Then, another slug struck him a glancing blow in the head, knocking him cold.

Earnest's 8-T-1 was the only Avenger still in the air. The expert Japanese pilots had flamed the others. It was only by a miracle that 8-T-1 had survived. The repeated runs on his plane had shredded Earnest's wings and fuselage. A 20-millimeter round had exploded behind Earnest, throwing shrapnel into his neck. The hydraulics were gone, and the elevator cables had been shot away. Still in a shallow dive, it looked like

(above) Long Island–native Sergeant Frank Melo. Although hit repeatedly and bleeding from wounds in his head, arms, legs, and side, Melo crawled through his B-26 to warn Muri that the plane was on fire and that everyone in the back of the plane had been injured.

they'd just impact on the water as Earnest struggled with the slack controls. Then he remembered the trim controls and worked furiously to bring the TBFs nose up. At the last possible second, he leveled out right above the waves, his Avenger a bloodied, Swiss-cheesed mess.

Ahead steamed a Japanese ship; he guessed it to be a cruiser. He pickled his torpedo at it and ran. The torpedo missed, but 8-T-1 survived. Earnest fled out the far side of the Japanese fleet, his compass and radio shot away, his instrument panel a broken wreck. He'd have to navigate by dead reckoning to get home, but at least he was alive.

Minutes after the TBFs were all but wiped out, Collins led his men into the buzz saw of the Japanese CAP. All

(right) The *Akagi* in the 1930s before it had been modernized. Built on a battle cruiser hull, it became the flagship of the carrier force and home to the best of Japan's naval aviators. When it was modernized prior to the war, the lower flight deck was removed and the main flight deck extended to almost the full length of the hull.

around the big B-26s, the sky soon filled with diving Zeroes, leading edges of their wing's alight as they triggered off bursts from their 20-millimeter cannons.

Collins led the formation in evasive maneuvers. The Mitsubishis would attack, and the Marauders would suddenly dip nose down for the waves, ducking out of the way at the last second. Still, they couldn't do this forever—they were running out of altitude.

The first hits smacked home. Ahead, the Japanese fleet loomed, and every warship in the formation seemed to open up at them. Soon towering water spouts kicked up by heavy shells studded the waters nearby. Throughout it, the B-26s dodged and weaved, speeding ever close to the carriers.

The Zeroes hung with them, ignoring their own flak to continue the pursuit. In the slot position, Lieutenant Jim Muri's B-26 lurched wildly as three Zeroes delivered a deadly volley of fire. Cannon and machine-gun rounds stitched the Marauder's fuselage, smashing the top turret and sending its gunner, John Gogoj, spinning into the waist position, flying shrapnel and Plexiglas fragments tearing his face to a bloody pulp.

Nearby, another Marauder took a direct hit in the left wing tank. A sheet of flame spewed forth and consumed the entire aircraft. It exploded seconds later, throwing bits of metal and debris all over the water's surface.

The fighters moved in for the kill, even as the remaining B-26s reached their attack points. It was the home stretch, and the race was on to see who would score next.

In Muri's B-26, things went from bad to worse. The Zeroes pressed their attacks with relentless efficiency, snapping out short, professional bursts at absolute point-blank range. In one pass, they chopped up the rear fuselage once again, wounding Gogoj again and sending the tail gunner, Earl Ashley, staggering back toward the waist gunner, Sergeant Frank Melo, with five bullets embedded in his legs.

Melo himself had just taken a hit in the head. Knocked senseless by the bullet, he clung with primal resolve to his .30-caliber machine gun, the fuselage around him pockmarked with holes and splattered with the blood of the three injured men.

Muri did everything he could to ruin the Zeroes' aim. He jinked and skidded and threw his Marauder into violent, quick turns even as he tried to set up for his attack. Behind him, all the gyrations flung his bleeding gunners about like rag dolls.

As Melo came to his senses, he realized the tail gun position had to be manned again. He crawled forward to get into it but was hit in the right arm as another fusillade of bullets ripped through the fuselage. He tried again, moving forward instinctively to defend his fellow crew mates. He hadn't gone far when a 20-millimeter shell exploded right next to him, sending shrapnel slicing through his side and legs.

Somehow, Melo made it to the tail gun. Clearing a jam, he got the guns working and brought them to bear on the pursuing Zeroes.

Another attack, more shells and bullets hacked away at the crippled bomber. A fire broke out in the tail gun position, and Melo's clothes ignited as he tried to throw a burning cushion overboard. He beat the flames out with

VMSB-241's surviving pilots and gunners pose for a photograph at Pearl Harbor in early July 1942 after their return from Midway. Quite understandably, they are a dispirited bunch. Sumner Whitten sits dead center in the group.

Significantly slower than the SBD, the 11 VMSB-241 Vindicator pilots soon fell far behind the rest of the squadron, led by Major Lofton Henderson. The SB2U possessed many deficiencies, including its limited payload of a single 500-pound bomb, but it did have a better endurance than the Dauntless. In fact, the Vindicators reached Midway earlier in the year by flying in nonstop from Pearl Harbor, a journey of at least 1,500 miles. The SB2U did not carry dive flaps either. Instead, the pilots were trained to drop their landing gear as they rolled into their dives. The drag they caused slowed the plane down enough to give the pilots time to aim and launch their bombs.

his bare hands, and then crawled back forward through the growing blaze.

They made it to their release point and dropped their torpedo just after Collins' crew released theirs—at least they thought they did, as the ad hoc release mechanism installed just before the mission didn't give them any sign that the torpedo had fallen away. None of the crew felt the aircraft lighten.

Collins broke hard right. Muri went left. As they came off target, Lieutenant Herb Mayes pounded across the wave tops straight at the *Akagi*. Mayes' Marauder barreled right over the bridge, missing the superstructure by a matter of

feet to the stunned surprise of several Japanese torpedo bomber pilots standing nearby, including Pearl Harbor veterans Shigeharu Murata and Mitsuo Fuchida. As it cleared the flight deck, flak finally clawed it down. Mayes and his crew died in a sudden inferno as their Marauder careened into the water a few yards off the *Akagi*'s beam.

Muri's crew wasn't out of the woods yet. They ran through the Japanese formation, hugging the wave tops trailing a cloud of pursuing Zeroes.

Bleeding from his head, arm, side, and legs, Melo appeared on the flight deck and shook Muri's shoulder. The young pilot turned, an unlit cigarette dangling between his lips, to see his gunner covered in blood and gore. Melo gasped out a report, telling him that the plane was afire aft and that all the gunners were down.

Pete Moore unhooked himself from his belts and climbed out of the copilot seat to give first aid to Melo, who passed out on the floor behind the pilot's seat. Moore then headed aft to put out the fires and administer first aid to the other two gunners. When he finished, desperate times required desperate measures: Moore climbed into the scorched and blood-stained tail gunner's seat and began snapping out bursts at the Zeroes still in pursuit.

Mercifully, their ordeal ended a few minutes later as the Zeroes finally gave up the chase. In the cockpit, Muri gagged. At some point during the attack, he'd bitten his cigarette clean in half and swallowed the filter.

He turned for Midway, his savaged B-26 more sieve than airplane.

Fifty minutes later, VMSB-241 reached the Kido Butai. Once again, the Zero CAP was ready for the Americans. The SBDs, flying alone and unsupported far ahead of the Vindicators, got the worst of it. The Zeroes rolled in on them and chopped half of the Dauntless dive bombers out of the formation. The sky was streaked with the death trails of flaming SBDs as they plummeted down into the stark azure Pacific.

The SBDs weaved and jinked but could not shake the Zeroes, who closed with terrier-like tenacity to point-blank range to hammer one SBD after another with cannon and machine-gun fire.

Captain Arnold DeLalio watched as one Zero swooped down from above and ahead of his formation. The Zero poured a long burst into the Dauntless in front of him, and then flashed past at high speed. The stricken Dauntless, flown by 2nd Lieutenant Tom Gratzek, rolled over and dove in, its engine and fuselage shrouded in flames.

And then they were over a carrier, flak blackening the sky around them. The survivors winged over and slanted down after their prey, the carrier *Hiryu*. Though the marines pressed their attack with extreme élan, not a bomb found its mark. Half their number gone, their leader Major Henderson dead, the survivors scattered on the wave tops and sped for home.

In came the Vindicators. Zeroes pounced on them like angry hornets, buzzing around and through their huddled formations. It was an uneven contest. The old, SB2Us should have long since been retired to stateside training commands, but equipment shortages in the fleet meant the marines would go in with the navy's castaways.

In the rear of the formation, 2nd Lieutenant Sumner Whitten watched as a pair of Zeroes made runs on his aircraft. Whitten was a northeasterner, tall and eloquent. He had more flight time in SB2Us than most of the other men in the squadron, but all his experience couldn't prepare him for what he faced that day.

In the first pass, the Zeroes killed Danny Cummings' gunner. Whitten looked over at his wingman to see the man slumped over his guns, one arm dangling overboard, a streak of crimson staining the side of the fuselage beyond his lifeless fingers. Cummings went in, but was later rescued at sea and lived to fight again at Guadalcanal.

Soon after the Zeroes intercepted, Jay Manning was killed in the turret of 8-T-1. This post-strike photo shows the damage to his station.

would fall to Ferrier to pack up the personal effects of the gunners lost. It was a lonely task, and one that Ferrier would never forget.

Muri brought his crippled B-26 back and mushed onto the runway. When it skidded to a stop, the plane bled fluids from dozens of jagged holes. Soon, oil and hydraulic fluid pooled together under its wings.

Melo and the other gunners were pulled gingerly from the bloody wreckage in the tail and taken to the base hospital. Collins and his crew were the only others to return from the B-26 strike. Both Marauders had been reduced to so much mangled aluminum. The survivors grabbed rifles and reported as infantry.

The marines weren't through. Though half the squadron had been wiped out, the surviving SBDs and SB2Us went out later that afternoon hunting for a reported burning carrier. Their new commanding officer, Major Norris, disappeared on that flight. The next day, during an attack on the

They were five miles from the carriers. They might as well have been on the moon. There was no getting through the Zeroes. Whitten's gunner banged away at them, defending his tail. In his excitement, he accidentally creased his own rudder—miraculously the only damage their Vindicator suffered in the entire attack.

Major Norris led them down into a scud layer. At 1,800 feet, they broke through near the battleship *Haruna*. The carriers, off in the distance, would not be reached by these aging dive bombers.

The pilots dropped as best they could. The survivors later reported at least two hits among the fierce anti-aircraft fire. Whitten had one glancing look off at the carriers and thought for sure Henderson's boys had hit at least one.

It was wishful thinking. Aside from a few near misses, the entire Kido Butai remained intact. Midway had shot its bolt.

Later that morning, the survivors straggled home. Bert Earnest, through brilliant navigation, brought 8-T-1 in with almost 70 bullet, flak, and cannon holes scarring the Avenger. He spun off the runway and came to rest in the sand, where he and Harry Ferrier emerged, the only men left from VT-8's Midway detachment. In a few days, it

The *Mikuma* burns fiercely and is only a few hours away from sinking. She was the last Japanese ship sunk at the Battle of Midway.

Mikuma, Norris' replacement crash-dived onto the cruiser's after turret and earned a posthumous Medal of Honor. The squadron lost three commanders in three missions.

Midway saw the first time the three services attempted an aerial attack together. It ended in utter failure, and few men survived. Poor training, terrible communication, and the vastly different cruising speeds of each aircraft ensured there would be no coordinated strike. Without fighter escort, the well-blooded veterans of the Kido Butai hacked their piecemeal attacks out of the sky. In later months and years, the services would learn how to make joint attacks work, but here at the birth of such complicated endeavors, the pioneers paid dearly for all the mistakes.

When the battle came to an end, Whitten stood alone on the beach, looking out over the breaking surf. Time and again, he returned to the same thought: "If all these missions will be this rough, how are any of us going to make it home?"

The *Yorktown* burns after the *Hiryu*'s bombers struck it in the early afternoon of June 4, 1942. Dead in the water following a second air attack, a Japanese submarine subsequently sunk the *Yorktown*.

Chapter Five

A Torch to the 4th Air Group

LIEUTENANT SHIGERU KOTANI HAD LESS THAN TEN MINUTES TO LIVE. A senior division officer (Buntaicho) from the Rabaul-based 4th Air Group, on the morning of August 8, 1942, he had led 26 Mitsubishi G4M Type 1 "Betty" bombers on a search-and-strike mission against the American warships in the southern Solomons. For over three hours, Kotani and his men had slowly cruised down the northern side of the Solomon chain, hoping to receive a radio report giving the location of the ever-important American carriers known to be somewhere in the area. Ahead of them, five big Kawanishi H8K "Emily" flying boats combed the sea north and east of Guadalcanal, ready to fire off a contract report at the first sight of American wakes.

No luck—the Japanese were looking in the wrong place. The American flat-tops were actually southeast of Guadalcanal. A twist of fate had sent one of the Emily's passing down northward of the American carrier force, but its crew failed to sight them.

(opposite) Australian coast watchers in the central Solomons spotted the Japanese G4Ms en route. They radioed a warning to the Allied fleet, and before the arrival of the 4th Air Group, the transports had weighed anchor and the warships had been organized into a very formidable anti-air screen.

The amphibious assault at Guadalcanal as seen from a U.S. Navy SBD. The attack caught the Japanese totally by surprise, but it did not take long for them to recover and start attacking the invasion force with both aircraft and later a surface task force.

Now, Kotani had a decision to make. He could continue southeastward, still hoping for a contact report while his escorting Zeroes began eating into their tiny fuel reserves. To do so risked the loss of those valuable Tainan Air Group pilots. Or, he could turn for Guadalcanal and attack his assigned secondary target, the American invasion fleet in Savo Sound.

The day before, the Americans had pulled off one of the great surprises of the Pacific War. Confident that they still retained the initiative in the Pacific, the Japanese were caught absolutely flat-footed when an Allied fleet suddenly appeared off Guadalcanal. Marines splashed ashore, and by the end of the day they had secured the partially constructed airfield there against only scattered opposition.

Meanwhile, at Rabaul, the Japanese reacted by sending the 4th Air Group down to bomb the invasion fleet. Its Betties had been about to launch an attack against Port Moresby when their target was summarily switched. They were not prepared, having armed their Betties with high-explosive

bombers better suited for airfields and land targets than for ships. The hastily launched attack did little damage to the Allied ships off Guadalcanal. So on the morning of August 8, the 4th prepared another attack. This time, its Betties would go in low, each armed with a deadly Type 91 torpedo slung under the fuselage. To get the planes ready for this mission, the 4th Air Group's ground crew had to remove the bomb bay doors from each G4M so that the torpedo rack could be properly installed and the weapon secured under the fuselage. It took time, but the 4th was determined to do this attack right.

Without carriers to attack, Kotani elected to go after the invasion force in Savo Sound. Several advantages lay with him and his men as they dropped their noses and headed for the waves on the northeast side of Florida Island. First, their route into the area took them down the north side of Santa Isabel Island, which masked their approach from Allied radar. Second, Kotani's men would attack on the deck, hugging the water as they worked through Savo Sound. The American combat air patrol had been sent to 17,000 feet. They would be too high at first to interfere with the attack.

The big Betty bombers roared over Florida Island, skimming the treetops as they followed the contours of the terrain back down to the southern coast. Twenty-three planes strong—three had aborted on the way—Kotani's men charged forward. His first chutai (squadron) took center stage, while his second chutai took station abreast of him on the left. His third chutai, nine planes from the Misawa Squadron, swung north and formed his right flank.

They greeted the Americans with a solid phalanx of speeding torpedo bombers. The pilots firewalled their throttles. Engines thundered and echoed across the placid waters of Savo Sound. In another age, they could have been cavalry charging heavy guns, a la the Light Brigade at Balaclava. It was a grand, sweeping sight.

At first, the sudden onslaught surprised the Americans. They had expected an attack and had sent their transports out into Savo Sound in four column lines abreast to be protected by a cordon of heavy and light cruisers along with eleven destroyers. Yet they had not counted on a low-level

One of the American heavy cruisers that provided the cordon around the vulnerable transports on August 8.

attack from the north and east. And at first, some of the ships held their fire, the crews believing the planes to be friendly.

The Australian cruiser *Canberra* disabused everyone of that error very quickly. Her gunners unleashed a torrent of anti-aircraft fire into the onrushing Betties. The anti-aircraft light cruiser USS *San Juan* soon followed suit, pumping out scores of 5-inch rounds from her 16 guns. Soon the heavy cruisers, including the USS *Vincennes*, opened up. With enormous blasts of smoke and fire, the cruisers cut loose with their main gun batteries. Soon, 8-inch shells kicked up huge water spouts among the wave-hugging Betties. To fly into one of those walls of water meant certain death, and at least one Japanese crew endured this fate.

The heavy flak caught Kotani off guard. The sky around his planes became pock-marked with black clouds from the exploding 5-inch shells. In the first five minutes of the attack, the American cruiser USS *Chicago* fired 142 5-inch shells and at least 2,000 rounds from its other guns. It was too much. Like a school of fish, Kotani's Betties veered left, and ran southward, hoping to find a gap in the Allied screen so they could get in among the transports.

The move made no tactical sense. Instead of charging the Allied warships at full speed, the Mitsubishi crews now presented their profiles as they moved parallel to them.

The gunners had a field day. A direct hit blasted one Betty to fragments. Pieces fell into the water. Another exploded in flames and cartwheeled across the waves. Yet another had its tail blown off.

The attack began to fragment. The flight leaders began to pick targets and turned to make a mad scramble into the Allied force. Flak clawed more of them out of the sky, littering Savo Sound with burning, smoking wreckage. Still, the Japanese crews held to their attacks. One Betty, wreathed in flames, tumbled into the water just aft of the *Vincennes*, blowing up only a few feet from the American cruiser. Another bored in, zoomed right past the *Vincennes'* bridge all guns blazing. Hoping and dodging, the G4M crew soared westward, aiming for the four columns of transports.

By now, the flak had taken a terrible toll. Only a few of the bombers remained. Among them was Kotani and his two wingmen. Somehow, they penetrated the Allied screen, evaded the counter-fire, and arrowed for the American transports. Only one emerged from the other side of the task force, fleeing west on the deck after completing its attack. The other two, including Kotani's crew, died in the hail of light ack-ack thrown up by the transports.

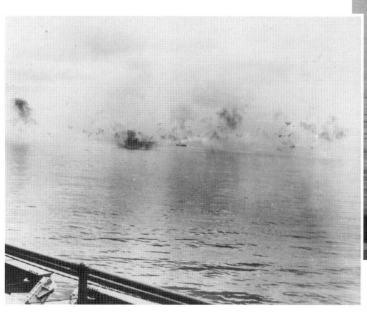

The Betties attack. Down low, they storm through intense anti-aircraft fire as they try to penetrate the screening cruisers and destroyers.

51

A flaming Betty slammed into the attack transport USS *George F. Elliot*. The bomber exploded near the ship's stack on the boat deck, spewing burning avgas in a flaming cascade throughout the ship. Liquid fire poured below decks, sparking fires everywhere. The flames soon reached the engine room and the *Elliot* lost power and steam. The calamity killed or wounded 45 men and forced the survivors to abandon their stricken, flaming ship.

Nearby, the USS *Barnett*, another transport, very nearly shared the same fate. A dying Betty's crew made a last-ditch effort to drive their broken plane into her hull. Instead, the plane tore through their rigging to plunge into the water only a few yards away.

One flight of three Betties singled out the cruiser *Australia*. The Aussie crew blazed away at their attackers with every gun that could bear. All three went down, but in one last act, the final G4M crew released their torpedo. It missed the *Australia* by a mere 30 yards.

Another Betty targeted the American destroyer USS *Jarvis*. A lucky torpedo struck home on the starboard side of the bridge. The blast crippled the tin can and stopped her dead in the water. The Japanese had drawn blood.

As the last of the attack unfolded, three American Wildcats from the USS *Enterprise*'s VF-6 appeared over Sealark Channel. They'd been far above the invasion fleet when the attack began. Now, they had speed and altitude on their side as they waded into a group of G4M's from Kotani's second chutai. The three Americans swatted down four Betties and a Zero with an inexperienced pilot who had tried to protect his charges.

Ten minutes later, the ragged survivors fled over the Western horizon. As the *George F. Elliot* drifted and burned, a quiet calm settled over the Allied fleet. For all its spectacular bravery, the Japanese attack had ultimately caused little damage.

Back at Rabaul, the tattered remains of the 4th Air Group reached Vanakanau Drome, where a crippled G4M crash landed. That night, the surviving crews dined with many empty seats around them. Seventeen of the 23 bombers that started the attack went down in Savo Sound. The one that

Only a few 4th Air Group G4Ms made it through the anti-aircraft fire. Down low, unable to avoid the massed flak from the Allied warships, they were swatted down one after another.

crashed back at Rabaul brought the total to 18. All five of the surviving planes were torn by shrapnel and rife with holes. In those brutal 10 minutes, 125 men from the 4th Air Group died or went missing.

Back in the sound, U.S. Navy ships picked up some of the missing. Altogether, the Americans pulled seven dazed and shocked Japanese aviators from the water. At least one crew elected not to be taken alive. The destroyer USS *Bagley* sighted the Betty that had had its tail blown off during the attack. Its broken fuselage had somehow managed to stay afloat. Turning to investigate, the ship's lookouts spotted several surviving crewmen sitting on the Betty's wing. As the destroyer pulled alongside to rescue the men, the Japanese began firing their pistols at the sailors lining the railing. They saved their last bullets for themselves. It was the Samurai way.

A Betty crashed into the transport *George F. Elliot*, setting it afire with flaming avgas. The transport burned through the night, and during the Battle of Savo Island, its glow illuminated the eastern horizon and in places silhouetted the patrolling Allied ships in the western and northwestern parts of the sound. A Japanese cruiser-destroyer task force used this to maximum effect during the disastrous night engagement known as the Battle of Savo Island. The Japanese destroyed four Allied cruisers before escaping with minimal damage.

One Betty blazed past the bridge of the cruiser USS *Vincennes* and strafed the bridge before ducking and weaving through the anti-aircraft fire as it ran for home.

One of the downed Betties afloat on the waters of Savo Sound. Its crew committed suicide rather than be taken prisoner.

Chapter Six

Murata's Last Charge: Battle of Santa Cruz

DEEP INSIDE THE *HORNET*'S STEEL HULL ON OCTOBER 26, 1942, THE DOCTORS WAITED. The loudspeaker had blared through sickbay only seconds before, announcing the arrival of attacking Japanese aircraft. Now, the deck quivered as the *Hornet*'s 5-inch guns opened fire. Sealed from the outside world by three decks and numerous hatches, the sickbay personnel were caught smack in the middle of a battle they could not see. Soon after the 5-inchers opened up, the rapid, dull boom...boom...boom of the ship's quad 1.1-inch mounts reached their ears. The aircraft were getting closer.

Being sealed inside a ship destined to be the primary target of any enemy attack was not for the faint of heart. Despite the occasional updates via loudspeaker, the men could

(opposite) The 5-inch .38-caliber DP guns formed the first line of the *Hornet*'s anti-aircraft defenses.

(right) The *Hornet* maneuvers during the outset of the first Japanese attack at the Battle of Santa Cruz.

only guess at what was happening above them. Their eyes were of little use, for there were no portholes through which to watch the onrushing attack. At best, they could only feel the progress of the battle through the deck vibrations and sounds of the great anti-aircraft batteries firing with reassuring steadiness. The wait as the bombers approached must have been agonizing.

A gigantic roar, a nearby explosion—the deck heaved and the men in sickbay struggled to stay on their feet. The blast came from up forward. What had happened?

Less than a minute later, two more explosions rocked the ship, one forward, one aft of sickbay. Before the men could recover from those two, a massive detonation assailed their ears and threw them off their feet. The deck lifted upward, as if the entire ship had been pulled like a toy out of the water. As the ship settled back down and the men tried to gather their wits, the bombers struck again. Two more thunderclaps split eardrums and sent the deck into violent contortions.

The familiar churn of the engines died away. The lights failed, cloaking sickbay in claustrophobic darkness. Then the cacophony of battle drained away. Sickbay was left in utter silence. It was unsettling that silence, for a healthy ship at sea always carries the hum of her engines through her hull.

In five minutes, attackers had battered their ship in a brutally efficient onslaught. Now she drifted, dead in the water, without power or communications. Fires raged forward and aft. Two Japanese D3A Val dive bombers burned below decks—kamikazes before they became vogue. Bomb hits scarred her decks, and below her waterline, two gaping holes gouged by torpedo hits had destroyed her most vital engineering spaces.

It was the last hurrah for Japan's elite prewar airmen— their greatest moment, but one that came at an unbearable price. For when the attack had ended, few Japanese planes escaped. The Imperial Navy's aerial rapier, the same weapon that had eviscerated the battle line at Pearl Harbor, had been shattered in one final charge to glory.

* * *

Lieutenant Commander Shigeharu Murata looked out over the American task force from 14,000 feet and knew he'd finally get a chance to attack an enemy fleet carrier.

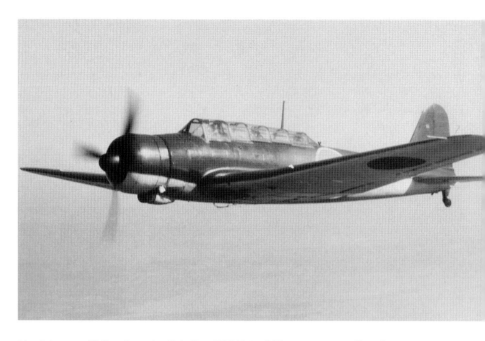

Murata's men still flew the aging Nakajima B5N Kate. Without armor or self-sealing tanks or even a forward-firing machine gun, the Kate proved terribly vulnerable to flak and fighters. Nevertheless, it remained the Imperial Japanese Navy's front line torpedo bomber until early 1944.

Perhaps the most experienced anti-shipping pilot in the world in October 1942, Murata's career had taken him from the deep recesses of China to the oil-soaked waters of Pearl Harbor. In 1937, he was one of two ringleaders responsible for the devastating attack on the USS *Panay* during the Battle of Nanking. He'd been a high-level bomber pilot then, a young and aggressive lieutenant with such an infectious sense of humor and affable nature that his fellow warriors nicknamed him "Butsu-San"—Buddha.

But his road to this one crowning moment of glory had not come easily. Murata had led the strike into Pearl Harbor and then followed the Kido Butai through its early strikes across the Pacific. With his close friend, Mitsuo Fuchida, in the observer's cockpit of his B5N Kate, he led the 180-plane strike against Tijilatap, Java, in early March 1942. Over the Allied naval base there, his Kate took a hit that ruptured his fuel tank. Unable to return to the *Akagi*, he headed for Borneo hoping to reach a friendly base. Out of fuel, his aircraft badly damaged, he crashed into the jungle with such impact that his gunner was killed instantly. After burying him, Murata and Fuchida wandered through the triple canopy jungle for three days without food. On the third day, they stumbled across their wrecked Kate and realized they'd been going in circles, slowly dying in the process. Somehow, they found a river and floated in its current until they finally came to a coastal settlement. There, a Chinese merchant allowed them to charter a junk. They sailed for Kendari, the nearest Japanese naval air base.

Two and a half months later, reunited with his men aboard the *Akagi*, Murata watched with none of his usual good humor as Collins' B-26 attack was pressed to the last aircraft. One B-26 barely missed the *Akagi*'s bridge before plummeting into the water only a few yards off her beam. While Fuchida and others cheered, Murata remained grim, as if he could foresee the *Akagi*'s ultimate fate that day.

Hours later, with the *Akagi* aflame from stem to stern, he abandoned the beloved flagship and floated around in the Pacific swells until rescued.

Murata had paid his dues, and now the payoff lay on the edge of the horizon. Finally . . . finally, he'd get his chance against an American flat-top.

He was with the *Shokaku* now, as its air group command-

er. It fell to Murata to lead this first strike of the day against the Americans. To get the job done, he had 20 *Shokaku* Kates and 21 *Zuikaku* D3A Val dive bombers. While he and the Kates cruised at 14,000, the Vals were stacked behind him at 17,000. Escorting Zeroes—14 altogether—covered both formations, ready to fend off whatever aerial attacks the Americans could deliver over the task force.

Forty-one bombers against the *Hornet* and her consorts, it would be a bitter fight to the finish, for Murata and his men knew the stakes. The fate of Japan rested on their ability to destroy the U.S. Navy's strategic mobility. The only way to do that was to nail the carriers. Success would be achieved at any cost.

Murata's radioman signaled the other planes to assume attack formation. Gradually, the Vals and Kates shuffled around until the Vals had formed a single column of three seven-plane chutais. Their eight escorting Zeroes took station 4,000 feet above and behind the Vals.

Meanwhile, the *Shokaku*'s 20 Kates split into two attack groups. The last nine B5Ns rolled to port led by Lieutenant Goro Washimi, who planned to bring his group down on the *Hornet*'s port side and deliver the classic anvil attack. Meanwhile, Murata took the other 11 Kates around to starboard and began a shallow dive toward their final attack altitude. He would lead his men around the opposite side of the American task force and hit the *Hornet* from the starboard side. The four Zeroes with the Kates stayed with Murata, leaving Washimi's group without any escort at all.

If all worked as planned, the *Hornet* would be dive bombed and torpedoed from both bows at the same time. The coordinated attack would prevent the *Hornet* from effective maneuver and split her anti-aircraft batteries. If they pulled it off, the *Hornet* would be sandwiched and destroyed in a matter of minutes.

The Vals drove straight in for the *Hornet* at the center of her screen of cruisers and destroyers. But as they ate up the distance

This is the volume of flak the *Zuikaku*'s Vals faced—5-inch fire thrown up by the anti-aircraft cruiser *San Juan*.

to their target, defending Wildcats climbed to intercept. Though totally outnumbered, two F4F pilots courageously waded into the Vals and in their first pass they left the lead D3A smoking and falling out of formation. This was Lieutenant Sadamu Takahashi's bomber, and though he jettisoned his bomb, his aircraft was too badly damaged to stay with his men. His Val fell away, its rudder jammed, and dove into a cloud.

Takahashi's chutai tried to stay with their leader, confused by his maneuvers. The remaining Vals drifted northward as their formation came unglued. For the moment, they were out of the fight.

Seconds later, more Wildcats arrived on the scene, and a wild melee enveloped the trailing two Val chutais. Before the Zeroes showed up to rescue them, the *Zuikaku*'s carrier bomber squadron had been thoroughly disrupted. More Wildcats joined the fray, savaging the trailing group of Vals. The American fighters crippled at least two Vals from this group, while possibly shooting down three more. With five out of seven knocked out of the fight, Takashi's third chutai had been all but destroyed.

Somehow, the middle chutai of Vals made it through the chaos relatively unscathed. Though one of their number fell out of formation trailing smoke after a Wildcat had made a pass on it, the other six huddled together behind their leader, Lieutenant Toshio Tsuda and bored in for the *Hornet*.

Tsuda's Vals reached the American screen. Two heavy cruisers, two anti-aircraft cruisers, and six destroyers could throw up more anti-aircraft fire than any of these veteran Japanese pilots had ever encountered. The sky turned black with 5-inch bursts, while bright tracers lit the sky in crisscrossing arcs. It was perhaps the densest concentration of anti-aircraft batteries yet seen in the Pacific War.

Thanks to the 5-inch .38-caliber dual-purpose guns, the killing zone began at 10,500 yards. For five minutes, Tsuda's Vals had to brave the torrent of flak as they descended to 12,000 feet and reached their tip-over points.

Tsuda led them down into a cloud. They fell out of the cloud's bottom at 5,000 feet, hardly the optimal setup for a dive-bombing attack. Nevertheless, Tsuda's chutai split up and rolled in on the *Hornet*.

At 0910, Tsuda made the first dive. Coming in from astern, he launched his bomb and pulled up just as his

(above) The Japanese dive-bombing attack begins. Quite possibly this photo captured Tsuda's near miss off the *Hornet*'s starboard bow.

(right) A *Zuikaku* Val passes low over the cruiser *Pensacola* following its run on the *Hornet*.

58

weapon exploded just off the *Hornet*'s starboard bow—a miss.

Behind Tsuda, Petty Officer 2nd Class Katsuhi Miyakashi came down to less than 1,500 feet. He held his nose on the *Hornet*'s bows and toggled his bomb. It fell with a piercing wail right onto the flight deck across from the island. It penetrated the flight deck, angling forward as it went through the hangar deck. Finally, three decks down it exploded in a messing compartment housing a repair party. The explosion killed or wounded 60 of the 65 men stationed there, creating a horrific scene made worse by the destruction of a nearby battle dressing station. The doctor assigned there was blown into a bulkhead so violently that the impact collapsed a lung. Now, as sailors lay dead and dying all around him, he could only look on with anguished frustration. His own wounds were too severe to allow him to do his duty. As Miyakashi completed his dive, Ichuro Kitamura howled down into his. Seconds after the first hit, Kitamura's Val was laced by anti-aircraft fire. The Val plunged straight into the water less than 10 yards off the *Hornet*'s starboard bow, its bomb still slung under the fuselage.

Next was Tsuda's final flight of three Vals. They would show the *Hornet* no mercy.

Leading this flight was Lieutenant (jg) Yozo Shimada. He sat in the Val's rear seat as his pilot, Petty Officer 1st Class Asataro Taka, winged over and pounced on the *Hornet*. A consummate professional, he ignored the light anti-aircraft streaming up at him and placed his bomb expertly on the flight deck aft of the island less than a minute after Miyakashi's hit.

The weapon detonated on impact, cratering the flight deck with an 11-foot hole and wiping out most of the men manning one of the 1.1-inch gun mounts. The shock wave proved so severe that it knocked a spare SBD down off the ceiling in the hangar deck, where it had been trussed.

Taka paid for his dedication. Pulling up low over the *Hornet*, Taka clawed for altitude right over the cruiser *Pensacola*. The gunners aboard that ship hammered away until the Val coughed up a long trail of smoke. The plane staggered and then stalled just as Shimada in the rear seat jumped clear. He parachuted to safety and spent the rest of the battle in the water watching the *Hornet*'s ordeal, but Taka rode the Type 99 bomber into the sea. It crashed

Heavy flak bursts from 5-inch anti-aircraft guns and studs the sky as the *Hornet* burns during the first Japanese attack.

about 1,000 yards away from the *Pensacola*.

The final two Vals followed Shimada and Taka down on the *Hornet*. One of the two planted another 250-kilogram armor-piercing bomb not far from the first hit. It penetrated deep inside the *Hornet*'s bowels before it blew up and knocked out one of the 5-inch ammunition hoists. Fortunately, nobody was killed.

Six Vals had just launched one of the most effective, if costly, dive-bombing attacks of the Pacific War. In 90 seconds of unleashed fury, they'd scored three hits and a near miss. They had nearly hit the *Hornet* with a doomed D3A as well.

The ordeal for the American carrier had just begun.

Off in the distance, the Hornet's gunnery officers could see the onrushing specks that belonged to Murata's *Shokaku* Kates. They were coming in on both sides, but even as the anti-aircraft guns began barking shells at them, more Vals swooped down on the stricken carrier.

These were stragglers from the lead chutai that Lieutenant (jg) Nobuo Yoneda had rounded up. He'd gathered the confused pilots up north of the American task force, but just as he led them around toward the *Hornet*, a

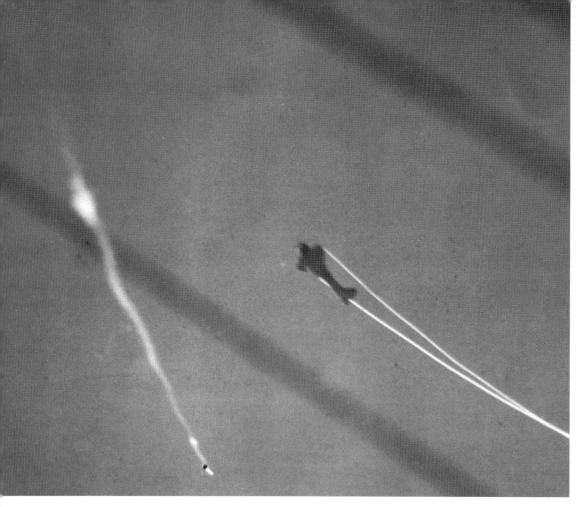

The *Zuikaku*'s second chutai diving on the *Hornet*.

right wing tearing through the signal halyards before grazing the ship's smokestack and breaking free from the fuselage. A fuel tank ruptured, spraying the signal bridge with flaming aviation fuel as the Val careened off the island and exploded on the flight deck. Sato's bomb fell into the companion way in front of one of Air Group 8's ready rooms, while part of his aircraft fractured the flight deck enough to prompt a rain of flaming avgas to stream into the ready rooms. Shaken, the reserve crews and pilots were forced to flee the liquid fire. It would be hours before this blaze was brought under control.

Seconds later, the *Hornet* was walloped by another enormous blow. Murata's torpedo bombers had scored.

While the American ships battled Takahashi's Vals, Murata had led his 11 Kates around intending to attack the *Hornet* from the starboard bow. But as the attack unfolded, the *Hornet* had changed course from 120 to 040 in order to get closer to the USS *Enterprise*'s task force off to the northeast. The course change spoiled Murata's attack. Strung out in a loose right echelon, the venerable old warrior suddenly found himself attacking from almost dead astern. This was the worst possible position from which to launch a torpedo attack, but Murata charged in. Off to his right, his three other chutais wheeled in toward the American ships in a loose arc from about 170 degrees to about 100 degrees from the *Hornet*'s starboard side.

Murata and his two wingmen made the first attack. Three hundred feet off the whitecaps, they penetrated the screen between the cruiser *Northhampton* and the destroyer USS *Anderson*. They were flak magnets, and as they roared toward their target, every nearby gun tracked and fired at them. Fifteen hundred yards from the *Hornet*, the gunners found their mark. One of the Kates took a hit, dropped its torpedo, and then burst into flames. It rolled over and spun

pack of Wildcats set on them. Led by Swede Vejtasa, late of VS-5 and then a fighter pilot with VF-10, the Wildcats managed to flame a damaged Val straggling behind Yoneda's makeshift formation. Vejtasa received credit for that kill.

Now only five strong, the Vals reached their push-over point even as the sky around them erupted with anti-aircraft fire.

The first four Vals dove and missed, their bombs sending up geysers of water on either side of the *Hornet*. Then at 0914, only a minute after the third bomb had struck the *Hornet*, Shigeo Sato nosed down and plunged after the American flat-top. Below him, as the deck welled up in his bombsight, desperate gunners poured a fusillade of fire up at his screaming Val. Flak ripped through his wings. He stayed on target. More hits rocked his Val. His nose never budged. Shrapnel slashed his fuselage. Fire erupted from the engine, and as flames licked along the Val's belly, Sato never flinched. Whether he was dead at the controls, or brave beyond reason will never be known. Either way, his crippled bomber slammed into the side of the island, its into the water—two Kates left. They held their course as bravely as their dive-bombing brethren. At 1,000 yards, the two remaining bombers pickled their torpedoes. They banked hard and turned to starboard, swooping toward the water to evade the relentless anti-aircraft fire that had chased them throughout the attack.

As they fled parallel to the big carrier, the gunners found the range. A shell tore into the left wing of one of the remaining Kates. The bomber staggered and started to roll to port as flames erupted along the side of the fuselage. It smacked into the waves right off the *Hornet*'s starboard side and exploded, leaving a greasy film of debris to mark its final resting place.

The last Kate fled across the American task force, trailing smoke. It escaped.

Murata did not survive the attack. His plane was probably the second Kate shot down. The great anti-shipping ace, whose career had spanned so many key historical events, died in the cockpit without ever knowing if he'd scored a hit on that most critical of targets, an American carrier.

Murata's flight of three scored two torpedo hits. The first Kate to release after it was hit probably missed. Murata and his remaining wingman braved the flak long enough to get in close. Their torpedoes ran hot, straight, and true right into the *Hornet*'s starboard side. The first one exploded below the waterline under the 1.1-inch anti-aircraft mount whose crew had been wiped out by the second bomb hit. It struck home at about 0914, mere seconds after Sato's Val exploded on the flight deck. The explosion ruptured the hull, sending water cascading into a number of anti-aircraft ammunition and powder magazines.

Less than half a minute later, the other torpedo exploded alongside the carrier's engineering spaces. This was the wound that ultimately proved fatal. With devastating effect, the torpedo's detonation flooded two fire rooms and ruptured one of the fuel oil bunkers. The stricken engineers suddenly found themselves bathed in a torrent of sea water and oil, and those who survived had to abandon their post. Soon, the forward engine room flooded, knocking out propulsion and power. The ship, darkened from bow to stern, began gliding to a stop.

Communications went down. All water pressure in the fire hoses was lost. The ship's crew resorted to fighting the growing conflagrations with buckets and chemicals by the hellish glow of the fires themselves mingled with the light of battle lanterns held by their comrades.

And still, the *Hornet*'s ordeal was not over.

So far, the attack had lasted five minutes.

Off the port quarter, a damaged Val appeared. Already streaming flames from multiple hits, probably by the intercepting Wildcats, the stricken craft executed a solo attack on the *Hornet*, but the pilot pitched his bomb into the sea ahead of the carrier. Pulling out over the starboard bow, the Val's pilot swung his nose around to port and circled ahead of the *Hornet*. Coming back around, he flew straight into the port side of the carrier near the forward gun gallery. The impact sheered its wings off, but the fuselage careened into the ship and skidded to a halt in the forward elevator pit in a spray of flaming avgas. The plane's crew died in agony as they roasted alive in their cockpit.

More Kates piled in for the kill. A minute after Murata's death, his second chutai penetrated the screen head of the destroyer *Anderson*. One of the Kates took a hit. The bomber wrenched upward as its torpedo fell free less than 100 yards from the destroyer. Blazing, the Kate heeled over to port and splashed down near the cruiser *Northhampton*.

One of Murata's last *Shokaku* Kates makes a courageous rush toward the *Hornet*'s starboard bow. Few of the 11 Kates from the starboard-side attack survived. Only four from the *Shokaku*'s entire squadron got home.

The remaining two Kates from this flight launched their fish and fled astern of the *Hornet*, running for the western side of the screen. Neither torpedo found its mark.

Three more of Murata's Kates made runs on the *Hornet*. Flak swatted down one, which hit the water ahead of the USS *Pensacola*. The other two dropped their torpedoes and escaped westward. Both pilots also missed.

On the extreme right, Murata's final chutai of two Kates tried to penetrate the screen. They had a very poor angle on the *Hornet*, and with the anti-aircraft fire so thick, their two-plane formation disintegrated. The leader, Warrant Officer Taneichi Nakai, blew past the screen ships and was heading for the *Hornet* when he changed his mind. He banked sharply and, skimming the waves, came back at the cruiser *Pensacola*'s port bow. He dropped his fish and escaped, only to be attacked on the way home by marauding Wildcats. He limped back to the *Shokaku*, his plane full of holes and his gunner dead at his weapon.

On the other side of the *Pensacola*, Nakai's wingman, Petty Officer 2nd Class Yoshihiko Kobayashi, elected to attack the cruiser as well, effectively creating a mini-anvil attack on the American ship. The *Pensacola* saw the threat and heeled to starboard, turning into Kobayashi's plane with all guns that could bear blazing away at it.

The volume of fire pumped into the sky could not be evaded. A thousand yards out, his Kate erupted in flames. Comet-like, it streaked straight for the *Pensacola*, flaming debris trailing in its wake. The bomber fell into the sea 100 yards off the cruiser's port bow.

Of Murata's 11 Kates, six survived the initial attack. Eight torpedoes had been dropped with two hits scored. On the other side of the task force, the other half of his anvil attack had just begun their runs.

Led by Lieutenant Goro Washimi, the nine remaining Kates suffered the profound misfortune of running into several F4F Wildcats. The American fighters slashed into the Kate formations and flamed two of the bombers while crippling another pair. One of the cripples was Washimi himself, who had to dump his torpedo. Rather than head for home as the other crippled Kate did, Washimi was determined to knock out the *Hornet*. He penetrated the screen and coaxed his dying plane forward. He almost made it. At 0918, less than a minute after the second Val struck the *Hornet*, Washimi's Kate crashed into the sea just shy of the *Hornet*'s port bow.

The remaining Kates fanned out through the screen and valiantly followed their doomed leader. Flak knocked another one down, but the four surviving crews, flying at about 200 to 300 feet, closed to point-blank range and dropped their torpedoes sharp on the *Hornet*'s port bow. Somehow, all four escaped, dodging and weaving through the flak as they ran for home.

All four torpedoes missed. Not that it mattered; the *Hornet* was now a doomed ship. With her engineering spaces wrecked, the crew could not restore power or propulsion. To be saved, she had to be towed out of harm's way. *Northampton* tried to do so, but the tow line broke.

Later that afternoon, as the carrier's dispirited sailors abandoned ship, several more air attacks added to the ship's woes, scoring several more bomb and torpedo hits. Unable to save her, the Americans tried to scuttle her with torpedoes fired from the destroyer *Anderson*. Though six more fish struck home, the proud flat-top remained afloat, lolling heavily in the Pacific's swells. *Anderson*, joined by the destroyer *Mustin*, then tried to sink her with a barrage from their 5-inch gun batteries. That sparked some new fires, but the 430 rounds that hit home also failed to sink her. *Mustin* and *Anderson* then turned and ran for safety, for as darkness approached, so did a Japanese surface task force.

Later that night, Japanese destroyers came across her hulk. Some consideration was given to trying to salvage her and take her under toe. Ultimately, the Japanese decided to simply sink her. Using their famed Long Lance torpedoes, the destroyers *Akigumo* and *Makigumo* finally sent the battered carrier to the bottom. The *Hornet* had died hard, but the first attack was the fatal blow that led to her ultimate destruction.

Murata had gotten his carrier. His men executed the last and best-coordinated attack on an American carrier during the Pacific War, securing three bomb hits, two suicide crash dives by Vals, and two torpedo hits in the space of five minutes. It was a frenzied attack made from practically every compass point, and the hits came with stark rapidity that must have been totally disorienting to the sailors below deck. One minute their ship was healthy and fighting hard. The next, she was a burning derelict. It was a masterful attack, one of the most professionally executed in the history of air-sea warfare.

Yet it came at a dreadful cost. Of the 41 Vals and Kates involved in the attack, only four Vals and four Kates

(above) The *Hornet* after the attack, dead in the water. A destroyer pulled alongside to help pull off the men abandoning their carrier.

(right) The men of the *Hornet* prepare to abandon their crippled, derelict ship. Japanese destroyers that came across her hulk later that evening sank her.

returned to their carriers. True, some of the downed crews were later rescued, including Shimada, who had witnessed the *Hornet*'s death struggle much as Ensign George Gay had seen the end of the Kido Butai at Midway. Nevertheless, the first attack on the *Hornet* virtually wiped out the *Zuikaku*'s carrier bomber squadron and the *Shokaku*'s torpedo squadron. Subsequent attacks on both the *Enterprise* and *Hornet* further denuded the Japanese carriers of aircrew and aircraft. When the battle ended, Japan's naval airpower was a blunted force. Gone were the expert pilots with years of experience. Gone were the crews who could execute complicated attacks even under the most grueling conditions. Gone were the pilots who were Japan's only hope. They had gotten their carrier, but they'd sacrificed themselves in the process. Those crews were Japan's national treasures, and with their loss went their irreplaceable skill and bravery. Never again would Japan's warriors seriously threaten the U.S. Navy. The balance of power in the Pacific had shifted. From here on out, the Americans would dictate the course of the war.

Part II

1943: STRANGULATION

WITH THE ALLIES DEVELOPING OFFENSIVES IN THE SOLOMONS AND NEW GUINEA, 1943 BECAME THE YEAR JAPAN'S FORWARD-MOST BASES WERE STRANGLED AND LEFT TO DIE ON THE VINE. This was done with a combination of expendable naval assets—neither side deployed anything larger than a heavy cruiser during the first 10 months of 1943—and air power. And, it was here that land-based air made its first stunning contribution to victory in the Pacific. General George Kenney's Fifth Air Force invented new tactics, field-modified their aircraft, and created the "commerce destroyer"—one of the most lethal anti-shipping weapons ever created. The commerce destroyers more than proved their value at Bismarck Sea, where they altered the strategic balance against the Japanese in New Guinea, setting the stage for MacArthur's offensive leap up the Northern New Guinea coast.

In 1943, the 5th Air Force's B-25 crews joined the ship-killer ranks with a vengeance. Rearmed with field-modified Mitchells, they employed new masthead attack tactics that decimated the Japanese sea lanes in the SWPA. Here, a 5th Air Force plane roars past a Japanese ASW escort off Kavieng as a cargo ship burns in the background. Note the bomb bouncing off the water at the bottom of the photo.

The 5th Air Force produced a host of ship-killers in 1943, including Lieutenant Thane Hecox, who sank a Japanese frigate at the entrance to Simpson Harbor on a low-level raid with the 345th Bomb Group on October 18, 1943. This two-photo sequence shows the results of his devastating attack.

Allied land-based air also played the key role in strangling Rabaul and Wewak, the primary Japanese base in the Southwest Pacific Area (SWPA). Through a grinding campaign of attrition, the Allies wore down the Japanese air units. As the Japanese lost control of the air, they lost control of their sea lanes as well. By midyear, few of their supply convoys could reach the South Pacific without first running a gauntlet of Allied air power. In desperation, the Japanese switched strategies and began moving their supplies on smaller vessels—luggers and "sea trucks." The Fifth Air Force feasted on these mini-convoys, sinking scores of them in barge-hunting sweeps along the New Guinea shoreline.

The culmination of the anti-shipping effort came at Rabaul in November. First, the Fifth Air Force launched a low-level surprise attack at the shipping resident in Simpson Harbor. That was quickly followed by the arrival of a new American carrier force into the SWPA that struck Rabaul with deadly accuracy twice, forcing the Japanese to abandon it as a fleet anchorage. By the end of the year, Japan could hardly move a ship in the SWPA without attracting an air attack and, as 1944 began, entire garrisons from Bougainville to Wewak faced utter starvation.

(*above*) Even the heavy bombers got into the skip-bombing act. Here, a 90th Bomb Group B-24 Liberator bounces a bomb into the side of a Japanese cargo ship off New Guinea in June 1943. The bomb is just about to strike the ship's hull.

(*left*) South Carolinian Captain Lyle Anacker, another 345th Bomb Group pilot, sank a freighter during an unescorted attack against Rabaul. He was killed in action.

Even barges weren't safe. Here, the A-20 Havocs of the 3rd Attack Group's 89th Squadron pulverize one of the "ant freight" convoys in New Guinea. With the larger ships taking so many losses to air attack, the Japanese tried to move supplies via coast-hugging barges throughout the SWPA. The 5th Air Force hunted them down ruthlessly.

Toward the end of 1943, the U.S. Navy's new fast carriers reached the Pacific. On November 5 and 11, their air groups attacked Rabaul and the warships anchored there. Here, a U.S. Navy dive-bomber pilot photographs the Japanese heavy cruiser *Chikuma* in Simpson Harbor during the November 11 attack. Several cruisers suffered severe damage in this engagement, and the Japanese withdrew them to Truk a short time later.

In early December, the fast carriers raided the Marshalls. Off Kwajalein Atoll, a formation of TBF and SB2C Helldivers damaged this *Kuma*-class light cruiser. That same day, the U.S. Navy flyers sank four cargo ships at Kwajalein.

A low-level U.S. Navy raid against a convoy in Kavieng Harbor, Christmas Day, 1943.

69

Chapter Seven

The Butchers of Bismarck Sea

G ENERAL GEORGE KENNEY WAS A PREWAR ODDBALL IN THE ARMY AIR FORCE. In the days when heavy bomber gurus preached the supremacy of high-altitude strategic bombing, Kenney passed his days raising hell all over the countryside with the 3rd Attack Group. He trained his men to fly low—so low that trees would spire above them as they practiced beating up airfields. For Kenney, the deck was the place to be. He loved the idea of hitting fast, hitting hard, all from below hangar level. It took discipline, courage, and just a touch of crazy. And he loved it.

While other careerists dreamed of great fleets of heavy bombers ravaging production centers, Kenney envisioned decimated troop columns, wrecked bridges, and airfields littered with broken aircraft. For him, flying wasn't flying unless it was done with the treetops above the canopy.

Kenney was a practical officer, and he knew attack aviation would need specialized weapons and tactics. He worked out the techniques, and then invented a low-altitude parachute fragmentation bomb, a perfect weapon against soft targets such as trucks and infantry or, better yet, grounded aircraft.

But years later, when he arrived in the southwest Pacific theater in the summer of 1942, he quickly realized what he needed was a way to sink ships. The Japanese had been moving convoys all around New Guinea, bringing in reinforcements and supplies that threatened the Allies' tenuous hold on Port Moresby. Time after time, Kenney sent his slender air assets against these ships, only to get inflated damage reports and little real results. The reason was the obsession with high-level bombing that had gripped the army air force before the war. Each mission saw Kenney's Flying Fortresses sortie against the Japanese ships and from 20,000 feet let go a string of bombs that did little but kill fish.

(opposite) A young Captain George Kenney, veteran of World War I's vicious air battles over the Western Front. He was one of the great interwar advocates for low-altitude strike aviation.

In January 1943, a 10-ship convoy sailed from Rabaul, bound for Lae carrying vital reinforcements, supplies, ammunition, and food. Kenney ordered his 5th Air Force to destroy it. Over the course of three days, the 5th launched piecemeal, ineffective attacks that succeeded only in sinking one ship. The others got through and delivered their cargo. Then, they sortied from Lae with seeming impunity and returned to Rabaul.

Kenney knew that another convoy like that would tip the delicate balance of power in New Guinea back into Japan's favor. This had to stop, and he was open to new ideas.

The answer lay in Kenney's roots—get low, get fast, hit hard.

Not long before this January convoy eluded destruction, some of Kenney's men had begun to modify their B-25 Mitchells. In a case of supreme serendipity, they belonged to Kenney's old love, the 3rd Attack Group. Now known officially as the 3rd Bomb Group (Light), they flew a mix of A-20 Havocs and B-25 Mitchells, some of which the crews had actually stolen from the Dutch in Australia back in 1942. These were men who had been repeatedly gut kicked by Japanese but refused to hit the mat. They were tough men, imbued with a sense of commitment to fight the Japanese at almost any cost in part because of the stories they'd heard of POWs tortured and airmen summarily executed.

In August 1942, the 3rd Attack sent eight Havocs against Lae. Zeroes and flak flamed six. The other two returned full of so many holes that upon landing, the commanding officer sent the survivors to Sydney on 30 days' leave.

Despite the defeats, the 3rd Attack possessed a spirit unmatched in the theater thanks to its excellent leadership. They also had a secret weapon in Pappy Gunn.

Pappy Gunn retired from the navy prior to Pearl Harbor and moved his family to the Philippines, where he ran a charter aviation company. In 1942, he escaped to Australia while his family was interned. Determined to do everything he could to hurt the Japanese, he attached himself to the local U.S. Army Air Force units and began offering engineering advice. By the time Kenney arrived, Gunn had become something of legend. An instinctive engineer, he came up with a way to up-gun the B-25 and make it a truly formidable weapon.

With Kenney's approval, he worked with the 3rd Attack's 90th Squadron and transformed their Mitchells into "commerce destroyers." After he finished, each plane sported four .50-caliber machine guns in the nose and four more in side packs on the fuselage under the cockpit. They started as factory standard B-25s. They emerged as gun ships with unparalleled firepower.

The new guns would surely prove useful in battle, but what the 3rd needed was a new way to hit ships. Bombing from medium altitude—8,000 to 10,000 feet—would never work. The bombers had to get down low.

Through the last months of 1942, the 5th Air Force had experimented with low-altitude skip-bombing attacks. In 1941, the RAF in the Mediterranean had used such a delivery method, and the Aussies had even tried it in the Pacific. They lost two out of three bombers in that attack. Simultaneously, the U.S. Army Air Force had experimented with skip bombing in the Everglades. The results were promising and, when the idea was posed to Kenney, he let his boys go off and try it.

The Flying Fort crews from the 19th and 43rd Bomb Groups made most of the initial attacks. In moonlit skies, they would sneak into Rabaul's Simpson Harbor and try to plant a couple of 500-pound bombs on the shipping anchored there. Using a big B-17 this way called for the kind of crazy courage that Kenney's leadership so often inspired in his men.

There had to be a better skip-bombing platform than the big Boeings. The B-25 was the answer, which is why the 90th Bomb Squadron became the 5th Air Force's designated anti-shipping outfit by early 1943. The B-25 was much more nimble and fast down low. When mated with the new skip-bombing tactics and the new forward-firing guns, a revolutionary new weapon was born.

Kenney wanted to ensure his new commerce destroyers would be used with maximum effect. Through January and February, his aircrew trained vigorously, knowing another convoy would soon sail for Lae. In effect, through the first two months of the new year, Kenney planned and prepared for what amounted to be the only set-piece aerial battle ever fought.

He knew the Japanese would send more reinforcements, and the Allies signal intelligence in the SWPA was so good that he knew he'd probably get advanced notice of the next convoy's departure date. In the meantime, his crews refined and practiced their new tactics.

Instead of piecemeal attacks, they would go in together with every available bomber. The B-17s would hit the Japanese from above, bombing from about 7,000 feet while the Aussies went in on the deck with their cannon-armed Beaufighters. Along with the Royal Australian Air Force (RAAF), the 90th would deliver the main attack with its new B-25 commerce destroyers. They'd strafe the ships, suppress the flak aboard them, and then rip their hulls open with devastating zero-altitude bomb runs. If all went well, they would go on the water and strike like cobras, just as Kenney had preached back in the days when he was a young junior officer.

Meanwhile, the 90th practiced its skip-bombing technique against an old prewar wreck in Port Moresby's harbor. This was no game—they used live bombs and lost one crew whose B-25 clipped the wreck's mast. Another caught fragments from its own bomb blast, a lesson the unit took to heart. In the future, delayed fused bombs would be employed, and the B-25s would space their runs out so they didn't run into their own blasts. They came up the learning curve fast.

On February 28, 1943, Kenney's 5th Air Force held a full dress rehearsal for the coming battle. Using the Moresby wreck again as the target, the 43rd Bomb Group's Flying Forts lumbered overhead at 8,000 feet. Close behind them was a squadron of B-25s, level bombing from 5,000 feet. These two attacks, while lower than usual, would be expected by the Japanese. This was how the army air force had operated for a year now.

But then came the surprises—props kicking up a froth of foam from the whitecaps, 30 Squadron RAAF Beaufighters barreled into the mock battle, all guns blazing. Behind this wall of cannon and .303-rounds came Captain Ed Larner and his 90th Squadron commerce destroyers.

The practice went off perfectly. Kenney and his men had grown together. They had not just thrown out the book; they'd set it on fire and cast the ashes to the wind. The days of bombing from the stratosphere were over. Through much effort and not a little blood, Kenney's men had learned how to orchestrate coordinated attacks. In the process, they had conceived a new doctrine on the fly and transformed their weapons to fit it. Now, they were set to unleash it upon the Japanese.

Jack Fox was a North American tech rep who worked closely with Pappy Gunn to modify the B-25s and improve their lethality. He is one of the unsung heroes of the air war in the SWPA.

***

The convoy sailed at midnight. Slipping through the black waters of Simpson Harbor, the eight destroyers and eight transports formed up and steamed along the north coast of New Britain. In the holds, the eight transports carried the bulk of the 51st Infantry Division and its equipment—6,000 men with artillery, anti-aircraft batteries, and plenty of ammunition. It was a force that, if it reached Lae, would make Buna look like a mere skirmish should the Allies attack.

They had to be stopped.

At first, the Japanese seemed to have luck on their side. Bad weather concealed the convoy as it moved west toward the Vitiaz Straits, where it would begin the most dangerous part of its journey and the final run for Lae's Huon Gulf.

But late on the afternoon of March 1, a 90th Bomb Group B-24 discovered the convoy and reported its location. Kenney put his men on alert. The battle would soon be joined, just as soon as the Japanese came into B-25 range.

In the meantime, the Liberators and Flying Forts would harass the convoy with traditional attacks while keeping tabs on its movements. The next day, the 43rd Bomb Group's B-17s delivered the first blow. From 6,500 feet—an altitude that would have horrified the prewar theorists— seven Forts emerged from the rain clouds and commenced their attack runs. Flak and fighters greeted them, but the gunners held the interceptors at bay while the bombardiers hunched over their Norden sights, knowing that every bomb counted this time.

Major Ed Scott and his wingmen Ed Staley and Francis Denault got it right this time. The Forts rarely hit anything but fish, and since the Philippines campaign the Japanese sailors held the big bombers in contempt. Why not? They had rarely caused any harm.

Not this time—Scott, Staley, and Denault stayed together while the rest of the B-17s launched individual runs. Together, their bombardiers pickled a quartet of bombs each. They howled downward and smothered the Kyokusei Maru. It was a masterful attack; at least five and possibly 10 of the 1,000-pounders struck home. The Kyokusei Maru never had a chance.

The bombs exploded across the length of the freighter, igniting raging fires that the crew could never hope to control. The ship was full of the 51st Division's ammunition and it was not long before it started to cook off. Each blast added to the misery of the crew and the battalion of 1,500 infantrymen who had boarded the ship at Rabaul.

The wounded died horribly, consumed in the flames as their countrymen flailed fruitlessly against the conflagrations. One bomb had struck among a company's headquarters group. All were immediately killed or incapacitated. Their comrades attempted to rescue them from the fire, but few were saved. The rest lay helpless on the deck, the flames to be their fate.

The Kyokusei Maru was a lost cause. As it burned and began to sink, the men aboard her began streaming over the sides. Most of the lifeboats had been destroyed in the attack, but that did not stop the artillerymen aboard her from salvaging two of their guns. They set them afloat on the remaining boats, determined to get their precious pieces to Lae despite this disaster.

Three B-17 crews—30 men—had just taken out the better part of a Japanese infantry regiment, an artillery regiment, and the ammunition supplies for both. Had they come ashore, it would have taken thousands of Allied troops to affect such damage—and at great cost.

The Forts escaped with only a few bullet holes. They'd fight again in the morning.

***

The Beaufighters attack. Practically clipping the masts of their targets, 30 Squadron paved the way for Ed Larner's commerce destroyers. In this scene, a Beaufighter crew strafes one of the seven remaining transports in the heart of the convoy.

Ed Larner's 90th Bomb Squadron wades into the convoy. A pair of B-25s roar over one of the Japanese cargo ships.

Dawn broke on March 3 to reveal the weather had abandoned the Japanese. They'd had the luxury of storm clouds through most of their voyage. Now, the skies were much clearer. Kenney's men would have no trouble finding the convoy.

At the airfields around Port Moresby, the crews were cocked and ready. They waited tensely at the flight line, pretending to read magazines or trying to play a board game with a friend. Old Victrolas offered up a melody of background music, but it failed to break the tension of the moment.

Just before 0900, the call came through. The convoy was running through the Vitiaz Straits, well within medium bomber range. It was time to execute the attack. Silently, the crews climbed aboard their bombers, probably unaware that they were about to change the course of the war in the SWPA.

They formed up over Cape Ward Hunt, RAAF Beaufighters and American Mitchells, Havocs, Lightnings, and Flying Forts. It was a polyglot force, less than 65 bombers strong. Nevertheless, the training and practice had welded them into a formidable strike force.

The bombers approached with 13 B-17s leading the way. Covered by 28 Lightnings, they ran into the Japanese combat air patrol and a dogfight played out across the sky around the heavies as they pushed on toward the convoy.

The Allied attack force split up to attack from multiple sides. The Japanese gunners looked on grimly, estimating that they were about to be hit by 50 planes. They hunkered down behind their weapons and prepared to do their duty. They had no idea what was about to happen to them.

The attack happened so quickly and with such violence that words can never do it justice. The Beaufighters dropped down from 500 feet and tore into the convoy, cannon and machine guns blazing. They shot up the decks and swarmed around the ships, dodging and weaving, guns chattering. Overhead, the B-17s rushed in and laid long strings of 500-pounders through the heart of the convoy. Seconds later, 13 B-25s from the 38th Bomb Group added to the chaos with a medium-altitude-level bombing attack.

The Japanese were simply overwhelmed. With bombers above them and Beaufighters strafing them, their return fire was split and ineffectual. And now, the main event arrived.

Ed Larner took his dozen commerce destroyers down to the wave tops. His men weren't convinced that this new form of attack wouldn't result in their own demise. They'd heard of Torpedo Eight and the decimation of the torpedo bombers at Midway and feared a replay here in the Bismarck Sea. John "Jock" Henebry, one of Larner's pilots that day, remembered the entire squadron was on edge. They were about to try something totally new and they had no idea what to expect.

In echelon right, they thundered upon the unsuspecting convoy, whose ships' captains thought them to be torpedo planes.

A mile out, as flak ripened in the sky around them, they unleashed their fifties. Ninety-six machine guns poured out 10 heavy rounds a second. And in that instant, the strafer was born.

The carnage was indescribable. Gun mounts were blown to slivers, their crews eviscerated and torn apart on the spot. Sailors and soldiers were cut to pieces as the fire walked along their decks. Holes were punched in their hulls, and more men died below decks and in the superstructures of the destroyers. Within seconds, Larner's men had crushed the convoy's ability to resist.

The 90th scores a hit. A Maru is bracketed by bombs as its stern anti-aircraft gun lies unmanned, probably as a result of the strafing the ship received.

Now it was time to get their bombs on target. Larner rolled left and arched around after a destroyer, his wingmen following until he told them to get lost and find their own targets. This tin can was his.

Twelve hundred yards out, Larner depressed the trigger mounted on the left handle of his control yoke. His eight fifties spewed bedlam. Aboard the destroyer, the sudden fusillade burst upon the ship with an intensity nobody had ever experienced. In seconds, the bridge was shattered, the men there sprawled like rag dolls as blood welled on the deck. Gun crews were vaporized, the decks swept clean of the living. The dead and dying lay in the fire's wake.

And then Larner's Mitchell was upon them. Far from launching a torpedo, the big bomber howled overhead and lobbed a pair of 500-pound bombs at the destroyer. One missed, but the other crashed through the after turret and detonated the magazine. The fearsome blast blew the entire stern off the ship. Amid its own oil and debris, the stricken destroyer sank.

Ed Larner had just taken out the convoy's flagship, the destroyer *Shirayuki*.

Larner pressed on, arrowing into the heart of the Japanese force, singling out the transport *Shin-Ai* Maru. His fifties flayed the new target, and fires sprung up all over its deck. Right on the waves now, the Maru swelled over him. Bare feet from his target, he pickled another bomb and pulled up almost through the ship's rigging and masts. The bomb struck home, gouging the transport that carried an anti-aircraft battalion, spare parts for the planes based at Lae, and some 1,052 soldiers and men.

After that run, Larner swung left and bored in on the destroyer *Asagumo*. He put his last bomb into her and headed for home. His attack was among the most destructive of the day.

The rest of the 90th Squadron strafed and bombed its way through the convoy. Behind them, they left flaming, broken ships in their wake. The path of the 90th could be traced directly by the incredible damage it inflicted. Altogether, they scored at least 15 bomb hits on three

A strafer's-eye view of the Japanese destroyer *Arashio* shortly before its destruction in the Bismarck Sea.

destroyers and all seven of the remaining transports. All were left afire and dead in the water, while Larner's destroyer had long since gone under.

Then, like a wedge of destruction, the 3rd Attack's A-20 squadron, the 89th, harvested the remaining ships with a fury. Guns chattered and bombs slammed home until 12 more hits were registered. The convoy had been ravaged.

Thousands of men ended up in the water, struggling among the oil and wreckage of a task force utterly smashed. The attack had lasted 15 minutes and had left all seven of the remaining transports sinking. Three of the eight escorting destroyers were badly damaged or had sunk. The 51st Division had ceased to exist as an organized unit, its soldiers reduced to castaways clinging to whatever flotsam they could find.

In the afternoon, the Americans returned and finished the job. The bombers pounded the remaining ships, sinking two more destroyers. With their bombs gone, they swung around and strafed the men in the water. Lifeboats, rafts, and bits of debris were blown to pieces as the guns churned the Bismarck Sea crimson. It was a sight that no man present would ever forget. Hundreds died in this unique killing zone. Even the B-17s swept low, the gunners spraying everything in their fields of fire.

Mercifully, it ended the next day.

In the course of the attack, Larner and the other masthead attackers had dropped 148 bombs against the 15 ships in the convoy. Forty-eight had found their mark. Kenney had found his ship-killers.

None of the food, ammunition, gasoline, and other vital supplies reached Lae. Only a few men, minus even their rifles, ever got ashore in New Guinea. Those who were saved by the four destroyers not sunk in the attacks returned to Rabaul as refugees with little but their clothing on their backs. And in some cases, not even that.

Others who survived the strafing onslaught floated through the Bismarck Sea for days. They died of thirst, they died of hunger, and they were attacked by sharks. Some drifted ashore, where natives and Allied patrols ruthlessly hunted them down. One boatload actually washed ashore at Guadalcanal. An American patrol killed them all.

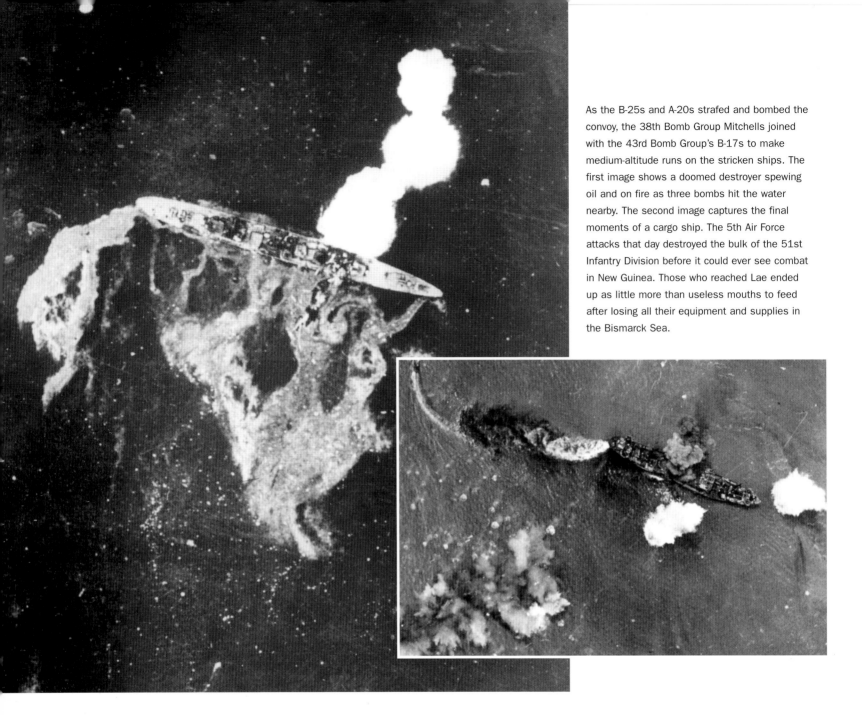

As the B-25s and A-20s strafed and bombed the convoy, the 38th Bomb Group Mitchells joined with the 43rd Bomb Group's B-17s to make medium-altitude runs on the stricken ships. The first image shows a doomed destroyer spewing oil and on fire as three bombs hit the water nearby. The second image captures the final moments of a cargo ship. The 5th Air Force attacks that day destroyed the bulk of the 51st Infantry Division before it could ever see combat in New Guinea. Those who reached Lae ended up as little more than useless mouths to feed after losing all their equipment and supplies in the Bismarck Sea.

Sixty-three bombers had destroyed an infantry division along with its attached elements. The cost was light—only a few planes and their crews. It was perhaps the cheapest strategic victory of the war, and certainly one of the most damaging. With the loss of the convoy, the Japanese at Lae were doomed. Few reinforcements and even few supplies would reach them, and the garrison began to die on the vine. When the Allies assaulted Lae by sea in September that year, they faced a fraction of the opposition they could have expected. The Battle of the Bismarck Sea had turned the tide in the southwest Pacific theater, ensuring the Japanese could not defend Papua New Guinea. Few victories, especially aerial ones, were as complete as the Bismarck Sea. Once again, the bomber crews had dictated the course of history.

(left) The low-altitude strafing and skip-bombing tactics caught the Japanese totally by surprise. The commerce destroyer B-25s and A-20s used the new tactics to their fullest effect and made quick work of the ships carrying the Japanese reinforcements to New Guinea.

(above) A 3rd Attack A-20 clips the mast of a cargo ship during the March 19, 1944, convoy battle off Wewak.

(right) A 38th Bomb Group B-25 about to kill a Japanese destroyer escort in Ormoc Bay in November 1944.

Chapter Eight

Bloody Tuesday

SEABISCUIT MAY HAVE BEEN THE FASTEST HORSE IN A GENERATION, BUT THAT NAME ALSO GRACED THE SIDE OF THE SLOWEST B-25 MITCHELL IN THE ENTIRE 5TH AIR FORCE. DICK ELLIS, A 23-YEAR-OLD SQUADRON LEADER IN THE 3RD ATTACK—THE YOUNGEST MAN TO HOLD THAT POSITION IN ALL OF 5TH BOMBER COMMAND—TOOK THE CONTROLS OF *SEABISCUIT* ON NOVEMBER 2, 1943, THE DAY THAT GENERAL GEORGE KENNEY'S MEN REMEMBER AS "BLOODY TUESDAY."

Rabaul was the target. That great Japanese base harbored the last surface striking force available to the Imperial Navy in the theater—a well-balanced force of heavy cruisers and fast destroyers. Simpson Harbor was one of the best natural anchorages in the Pacific, and at the beginning of November 1943 it housed dozens of transports, cargo ships, auxiliaries, and warships.

They needed to be knocked out. November 2 was the day.

After a morning full of weather delays, Kenney gave the word. The attack was a go. From all over eastern New Guinea, the 5th Air Force's bomber squadrons took flight and formed up. All the mediums that could fly would be in on this one. The 38th and 345th would strike the airfields around Simpson Harbor while laying a curtain of smoke with white phosphorous bombs in a way designed to mask the shore-based anti-aircraft batteries from the main attack against the ships in the harbor. It fell to the venerable 3rd Attack to execute that part of the mission.

(opposite) Dick Ellis stands under *Seabiscuit*'s nose. Ellis flew over 200 combat missions with the 3rd Attack and then returned home after the war to practice law in Wilmington, Delaware. Recalled to active duty in 1950, he stayed in the air force, where he served as the head of the Strategic Air Command.

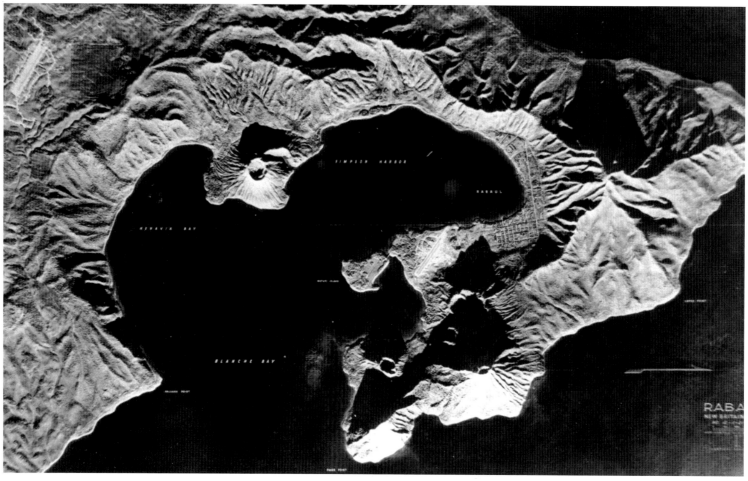

(left) A pair of P-38 Lightnings escorts a B-25 en route to Rabaul.

(below) A three-dimensional topographical map of Rabaul that the navy created for the strikes in November.

(opposite, above) More carnage on the airfields as the phosphorous bombs are released.

(opposite, below) The 3rd Attack in Simpson Harbor, strafing the shipping there as the attack unfolds.

Overhead, all of Kenney's precious P-38 units—the 80th, 39th, and 9th Fighter Squadrons, along with the 475th Fighter Group—would cover the bombers as they carried out their attacks. The Japanese still had a formidable fighter force defending Rabaul, and they would surely try to intercept with everything they had.

In Simpson Harbor that morning, Admiral Omori's striking force, consisting of the heavy cruisers *Myoko* and *Haguro*, a light cruiser, and several destroyers, dropped anchor after a brutal engagement off the coast of Bougainville. They'd lost the light cruiser *Sendai* in the last night surface action of the Solomons campaign only a few hours before. Omori's force had hoped to disrupt the American landings on Bougainville, but instead had the tables turned on them by a well-disciplined American cruiser and destroyer force.

The sailors, exhausted from the night's battle, set to work repairing the damage their ships had suffered in the engagement. Suddenly, the quiet of the afternoon was broken by the distant throb of aircraft engines. Lookouts scanned the skies. The Americans were coming. At the nearby airfields, pilots raced to their waiting fighters in a mad scramble to get aloft before they could be destroyed on the ground.

Two squadrons of P-38s streamed over Simpson Harbor, paving the way for the medium bombers a few minutes behind. The Zeroes they spotted were swatted down, but more lifted from the strips at Lakunai and Vunakanau. The air soon buzzed with their angry Sakae engines.

And then, the mediums arrived. The 38th and 345th raged on the scene, guns blazing as they shot up the town and the local airfields. Phosphorous bombs exploded into awesome white mushroom clouds, tendrils of smoke streaking out to every compass point. The airfields were killing zones that afternoon, as hundreds of concentrated machine guns hammered away at the aircraft and installations. Parafrags—Kenney's personal invention—tumbled out of bomb bays to spread halos of shrapnel-torn destruction across the fields. No aircraft or human could survive in their blast zones.

Into this inferno came the 3rd Attack. Sweeping down from the north, hugging the mountains and the volcanic crater nearby, they charged line abreast, noses aflame as they strafed everything to their front.

The sky was scarred with hundreds of flak bursts. Aircraft cartwheeled earthward in flames. General John "Jock" Henebry's bombers skimmed the smoke and tore into the harbor as the 9th Fighter Squadron fought hard to keep the Zeroes off their backs.

The 3rd Attack split up, the pilots picking their targets as their engines dragged them along at 230 miles per hour indicated. Behind them lagged Dick Ellis and *Seabiscuit*, whose aging engines screamed in protest as its pilots fire-walled the throttles.

The scene in Simpson Harbor from the rear of Henebry's B-25. In the background, the first cargo ship Henebry attacked burns. The second one in line has just taken a hit amidships. The heavy cruiser *Haguro* is anchored close by. The forward 8-inch gun turrets have been trained out to port and are about to start shooting at Dick Ellis in *Seabiscuit*.

Ellis joined the battle as ahead Henebry released on a cargo ship, his guns churning the deck to splinters. His first bomb, a 1,000-pounder, skipped off the water only a few yards shy of the target ship and slammed into the side of its hull. A split second later, it detonated deep inside the ship, just as Henebry pulled up hard to avoid hitting his target's mast.

Colonel John Henebry (at right) took his B-25, *Notre Dame de Victoire*, into Simpson Harbor on Bloody Tuesday and struck two cargo ships, sending one to the bottom before he'd even completed his attack. Standing in the middle is Major Gerald R. Johnson, the commander of the 9th Fighter Squadron and leader of the fighter escort protecting Henebry's 3rd Attack that day over Rabaul.

Ahead, he spotted another Maru—a big one that he later guessed to be 10,000 tons. Hard on the yoke, he pushed his B-25's nose down and unleashed his fifties. Their bullets struck the Japanese ship with blistering effect, even as Henebry set up for a skip-bombing run. Props only inches off the harbor surface, he flung his B-25 right at the Maru and toggled his next bomb. It skipped across the waves while he hauled back on the yoke. The Mitchell sped skyward, its nose high as it blasted over the Maru. But here Henebry made a mistake.

On the other side of the cargo ship, the cruiser *Haguro* lay at anchor. He'd just exposed his belly to this deadly ship, and the Japanese gunners capitalized on the moment. Twenty-five-millimeter shells whipped past the cockpit on all sides. Henebry and his copilot Don Frye fought to bring the nose down so they could hose the cruiser with their fifties.

The Mitchell shuddered as 25-millimeter shells punched through the tail, rudders, and fuselage, tearing up the rear gunner's position and knocking out his twin fifties. Somehow, the gunner himself escaped harm.

Then they were over the *Haguro*, flashing past the big warship so low that Henebry clearly saw the captain standing on the bridge staring back at him, a pair of binoculars around his neck.

And then Henebry was through the worst of the flak, running hell bent for leather across the harbor. He dumped his last bomb, a 500-pounder, and stayed low. Keeping his damaged bird in the air soon became problematic. Engines damaged, tail a sieve, the pilots used every trick they had to coax their Mitchell along.

Chuck Howe followed Henebry into Simpson Harbor behind the controls of his B-25, *Here's Howe*. As he sprinted for the harbor, he broke left and went after another cargo ship. Howe sent two bombs down on it from below masthead height and hopped the freighter as the bombs did their deadly work. The crew saw one skip right into the hull, while the other bounced off the deck and exploded nearby.

Dick Ellis arrived on the scene about this time to the left of and behind Henebry, all guns raking the ships ahead. He picked out what was later called a destroyer tender and saturated it with .50-caliber fire before zooming overhead and sending a 500-pound bomb cascading into her hull. Then they too ran afoul of the *Haguro's* massed anti-aircraft batteries. *Seabiscuit* was off the *Haguro's* port bow, giving the 8-inch guns a clear field of fire. They opened up on the bomber with main battery fire. Fifty feet off the water, zipping along at about 250 miles per hour, Ellis sped past the cruiser. But before he got away from her deadly guns, his plane rocked violently as a near miss, possibly from one of the 8-inch turrets, exploded behind them. The force of the blast pushed the tail up, and for a second it looked as if the *'Biscuit* would be smashed to pieces on the wave tops. But Ellis and his copilot Johnny Dean masterfully recovered, pulling out with only a millisecond to spare.

Seabiscuit wasn't done yet. Ahead they spotted another freighter and Ellis galloped after it, seemingly oblivious to their near encounter with the afterlife. His left index finger jammed down on the gun tit. His fifties chugged and tracers raked across the freighter's length. Wings level now, the freighter loomed large in the windscreen and Ellis hit the bomb release button on the right handle of his control column. The Mitchell heaved up and over the Maru and *Seabiscuit* surged forward with a burst of unbridled speed. Ellis closed the bay doors and ran for home.

Behind him, the harbor was shrouded in smoke and flames.

But the egress wasn't easy. Fighters dogged both Henebry and Ellis, shooting up both and damaging *Seabiscuit's* right engine.

They limped home to Kiriwina, where Henebry ditched his bird in the surf. Ellis brought *Seabiscuit* down safely, as did Chuck Howe in *Here's Howe*. But it had been a costly mission. Eight B-25s and nine P-38s went down over the harbor, and many of those that got home weren't worth saving. They were pushed into the local bone yards and stripped for parts. Forty-five members of fighter and bomber crews died or went missing in what became the largest single air battle fought by the 5th Air Force in the SWPA. Seventy-eight B-25s were launched from New Guinea, covered by 70 P-38s. For the Pacific in 1943, that was an enormous raid.

And what of the damage the 3rd Attack inflicted? The 5th Air Force concluded that at least two destroyers, one destroyer tender, eight Marus, and a quartet of small luggers had been destroyed. Kenney considered it a tremendous victory, one so significant his 5th Air Force PR officers put together a photo book to commemorate the occasion. It was sent with a personal note to the families of every 5th Air Force man on the raid.

More destruction in the harbor. Postwar investigations by the Strategic Bombing Survey found that two large transports and six other cargo ships had been sunk by the 3rd Attack Group on November 2, 1943.

Part III

1944:
CLEAN SWEEP

AT THE END OF 1943, THE U.S. NAVY UNLEASHED ITS CENTRAL PACIFIC OFFENSIVE WITH THE NEW ESSEX-CLASS FAST FLEET CARRIERS AT ITS HEART. After the conquest of Tarawa in the Gilberts, the navy and marines moved into the Marshalls, and then made the leap into the Marianas by midyear. The new carrier fleet offered unparalleled strategic mobility and enough firepower to devastate even the most heavily defended Japanese bases. Truk was hit twice in the first months of 1944, destroying it as a viable forward base for the Imperial Navy. Finally, in June, the Japanese tried to counter the marauding American flat-tops. In the Battle of the Philippine Sea, the Imperial Navy risked its reconstituted carrier force in a chaotic, two-day battle. When it was over, Japan had lost three flat-tops (two to submarines) and almost all its carrier-based aircraft. The forces that the Japanese spent a year rebuilding had been destroyed in 48 hours.

(opposite) A small freighter is strafed in Victoria Bay. The 5th Air Force began 1944 as it ended 1943, destroying Japan's shipping traffic between New Guinea and the rest of the Empire.

The 38th Bomb Group attacks a Japanese freighter off Sorong, June 17, 1944.

Meanwhile, the U.S. Army Air Force unleashed a series of destructive attacks on the last of the Japanese supply lines in New Guinea. In March, the Fifth Air Force wiped out a convoy off Wewak. The scene was repeated again off Manokwari in June. By midyear, nothing but submarines could bring supplies to the 200,000 Japanese troops in New Guinea. The Fifth Air Force completed the strangulation of an army almost as large as the one that the Soviets destroyed at Stalingrad.

In October, the Americans returned to the Philippines, triggering a succession of air-sea battles that started with the Battle of Leyte Gulf. In what became the largest naval battle in history, the Japanese fleet suffered catastrophic losses to air attack and surface engagements. By October 25, the Imperial Navy had been crushed and would never pose a serious threat to the Allies again. The last of the Japanese battleships and carriers returned to Japan, where most sought refuge in Kure Harbor.

The final two months of the year witnessed a succession of fierce air-sea clashes in the Philippines. First, the navy and army air force launched a series of mopping-up attacks on the fleeing imperial fleet after Leyte Gulf. Off Manila Bay, Air Group 19, the destructors of the carrier *Zuikaku*, caught the heavy cruiser *Nachi* and sent her to the bottom. Other ships followed. Later, a number of convoy battles erupted around Leyte as the Japanese sought to reinforce its garrison there. Initially successful, the U.S. Army Air Force and U.S. Navy finally deployed enough air assets to crush the remaining convoys. Leyte was cut off and strangled, though the fighting in its muddy jungle mountains continued into 1945.

During 1944, the Allies swept the seas clean of the Imperial Navy. With the Americans ascendant, the Japanese homeland would soon come under attack.

A close-up of the same freighter as a strafer B-25 hammers it with .50-caliber machine-gun fire.

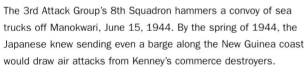

The 3rd Attack Group's 8th Squadron hammers a convoy of sea trucks off Manokwari, June 15, 1944. By the spring of 1944, the Japanese knew sending even a barge along the New Guinea coast would draw air attacks from Kenney's commerce destroyers.

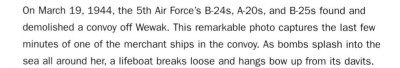

On March 19, 1944, the 5th Air Force's B-24s, A-20s, and B-25s found and demolished a convoy off Wewak. This remarkable photo captures the last few minutes of one of the merchant ships in the convoy. As bombs splash into the sea all around her, a lifeboat breaks loose and hangs bow up from its davits.

(above) A merchant ship, probably loaded with ammunition, explodes off Truk during an attack by planes from the USS *Enterprise*.

(left) While the 5th Air Force ravaged Japan's SWPA convoy lanes, the U.S. Navy unleashed its central Pacific offensive. After securing the Gilberts, the navy and marines attacked and captured key atolls in the Marshalls in February. To support that operation, the fast carriers struck Truk on February 17, 1944. The anti-ship strikes sunk or damaged almost 50 ships in Truk lagoon. Other ships were caught running from the atoll and attacked in the open sea. Here, a navy TBF comes off target after completing a run against a destroyer off Truk the day before the main attacks.

91

Ship-killing on a macro scale. In November, the fast carriers launched a punishing series of raids against Japanese shipping in Manila Bay. These photographs clearly show the ferocity and effectiveness of those attacks.

A Japanese B6N Tenzan "Jill" torpedo bomber—
the Kate's replacement—launches a solo torpedo attack against the *Essex* off Formosa a few
weeks before the Battle of Leyte Gulf.

U.S. Navy search aircraft discovered the heavy cruiser *Nachi* off Manila Bay on November 5, 1944. Air Group 19 off the *Lexington* spearheaded the attack on the warship and played the key role in sending her to the bottom. A few months later, navy divers recovered a host of code books from the *Nachi*, and these documents played a key role in naval signal intelligence operations for the rest of the war. In the series of photographs, dive and torpedo bombers hit the *Nachi*. Three torpedo tracks streak for the doomed cruiser.

The 341st skip-bombs ships in Hong Kong's Victoria Harbor in December 1944. The 341st used their strafers to launch crippling attacks on Japanese convoys and harbors.

Chapter Nine

First Licks,
Last Licks

ON OCTOBER 24, 1944, AIR GROUP 20 DREW THE MORNING SEARCH OFF NEGROS ISLAND. Its pilots and crews climbed into their Avengers and Hellcats, formed into two search-and-strike elements of six Curtiss SB2C Helldivers and eight Grumman F6F Hellcats each and headed southwest across Leyte Gulf in search of the Japanese fleet.

Everyone knew the Japanese fleet had sortied. Its last carriers, battleships, cruisers, and destroyers had been sent in motion the moment the Americans invaded Leyte. The Imperial Navy had already suffered significant losses—patrolling submarines had sunk four heavy cruisers. Undeterred, the remaining elements, broken into three groups, steamed hard for the American invasion force.

Now, on the morning of October 24, the Americans sent aloft a vast search force to comb the seas and passages through the Philippines.

And as fate would have it, the *Enterprise*'s bold pilots found the southern force. At about 0830, Lieutenant Ray Moore discovered two battleships and their escorting consorts about 50 miles off the southwest part of Negros Island and at the edge of their endurance.

Moore called in the troops and leaned out his fuel mixture. He'd be in the area for a while. He began to orbit, as the rest of the Big E's aircraft gathered around him.

(opposite) Air Group 20's search-strike located the Japanese southern force on the morning of October 24, 1944. After gathering its 28 planes from their assigned search areas, the *Enterprise*'s flyers dove to the attack. Taken shortly after 0915, this photograph shows the battleship *Fuso* under attack. The Big E's planes scored a hit on the stern of the old battlewagon that did little damage. Nonetheless, this was the first ship strike against the onrushing Japanese battleship forces at Leyte Gulf.

The *Fuso* and *Yamashiro* evade Air Group 20's attacks on the morning of October 24.

Kurita's force under attack in the Sibuyan Sea. At left, either the *Musashi* or the *Yamato* turns hard to port.

It didn't take long for the rest of the search planes to arrive. Together, they formed up and swung around the Japanese ships until they took up position up sun from them. With the entire force together, VB-20's commanding officer Emmett Riera took the lead. He called out targets for his bombers and asked VF-20's skipper, Fred Bakutis, to take the Hellcats down on flak-suppressing runs against the escorts.

Just after 0900, this little force of 28 planes rolled in on the battleships *Fuso* and *Yamashiro*. Ten miles out, the sky suddenly filled with a crazy quilt of colored flak—purple, red, yellow, white, and blue puffs of smoke mushroomed around them. As they closed, phosphorous shells came streaking up after them, adding to the dizzying barrage of ack-ack the likes of which none of the pilots had ever seen.

The Hellcats went in first, mimicking the role of the now disbanded Scout Bombing Squadrons. Prewar doctrine had called for the scout bombers to pave the way for the main attack with their 500-pound bombs. By splitting the defensive fire and suppressing it where possible, the ships theoretically would be unable to fight off the bombing and torpedo squadrons. Now, after two years of combat, that role fell to the fighter-bomber F6Fs.

In 60-degree dives, they rocketed and strafed the escorting ships. Somebody planted a rocket right on the destroyer *Shigure*'s forward turret. The blast killed the gun crew and disabled the turret. It was a remarkable hit, as the *Shigure*'s

crew was as experienced as they came, having fought in almost every battle during the Solomons campaign the year before.

As the F6Fs pulled off target, the Helldivers fell out of the sky from 15,000 feet.

The *Fuso* and *Yamashiro* threw up an incredible amount of flak, but they failed to deter Bombing 20. The pilots held their Beasts steady and pickled off their two 500-pound bombs at 2,000 feet, strafing all the way down with their 20-millimeter wing-mounted cannons.

The Helldiver pilots thought they'd scored several hits on one battleship, sparking a small fire on her stern. The other appeared to be burning midship as they climbed back up and headed for home. Not bad for a small search group with only 500-pound bombs.

In reality, the Bombing 20 scored a single hit on the battleship *Fuso*. The bomb exploded on the fantail and demolished all the ship's float planes, which probably made the American dive bomber pilot an instant ace. The *Yamashiro* was not hit.

Leyte Gulf's opening aerial blow had been delivered. The *Enterprise*, veteran of four carrier clashes, had gotten in first licks.

As the Big E's bombers readied their attack on the *Fuso*, search planes from Task Group 38.2, which included the carriers *Intrepid*, *Cabot*, and *Independence*, discovered the main Japanese surface task force. Commanded by Vice Admiral

Bombing 19's SB2C Helldivers on the deck of the *Lexington*, otherwise known as the *Blue Ghost*. On the 24th, the VB-19 was forced to attack Kurita's force with 500-pound general purpose (GP) bombs. They were not armor-piercing weapons and the crews knew they'd have little effect on the Japanese battlewagons.

Takeo Kurita and called the "Main Body" by the Japanese, it had been spotted near the southern tip of Mindoro as it sought entry into the Sibuyan Sea.

The Main Body included five battleships, the *Yamato*, *Musashi*, *Nagato*, *Haruna*, and *Kongo*. This would be the main target for the American carrier air groups, whose decks plowed the seas east of Samar and Luzon.

Task Group 38.2 launched the first attack of the day at 0926. Twenty-one Hellcats, 12 Helldivers from VB-18, and a dozen Avengers left the *Intrepid* and *Cabot* and sped toward the onrushing Japanese fleet. An hour later, they attacked through intense anti-aircraft fire. Bombing 18 off the *Intrepid* followed the Hellcats down as the TBM's split to make an anvil attack. The SB2C crews from VB-18 had been hit hard recently, losing almost half the squadron in three weeks of fighting. It still retained a core of veterans, including a couple of pilots who'd served on the *Yorktown* at Coral Sea and Midway. Their commander, George Ghesquire, led them down against the *Musashi*.

The flak was simply unbelievable. Seemingly every spare nook and cranny aboard the super-battleship had been packed with anti-aircraft mounts. Now, the sky grew so black with flak bursts that the pilots had trouble keeping their target in sight. The gunners began to score hits. One Helldiver after another caught fire and spun in. But the survivors had iron nerves and refused to be denied this once-in-a-lifetime opportunity. Releasing at point-blank range and then graying out during their 10-G pullouts, the men of Bombing 18 looked back on their target and were pleased to see smoke and flames boiling up as a result of their handiwork. They'd scored one hit with a 1,000-pounder, but had lost five SB2Cs—almost half the squadron.

More attacks followed. The second strike arrived at 1245, hitting the *Musashi* with another four torpedoes and four bombs.

For the crew of that monstrous warship, it would be a very, very long day. For most, it would be their last.

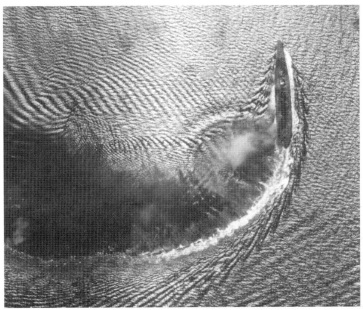

A dive-bomber pilot's view of the *Musashi* during the air-sea battle in the Sibuyan Sea.

The *Nagato* under attack. This battleship had been the flagship of the Combined Fleet until the *Yamato* was completed shortly after the start of the war. The *Nagato* was one of the few battleships to survive the war. Ultimately, she was expended during the Bikini atomic bomb tests in 1946.

While the bombing and torpedo squadrons focused on the Japanese battlewagons, rocket and bomb-equipped F6F Hellcats tried to suppress the destroyers and cruisers with 60-degree diving attacks. Here, a Japanese destroyer takes a number of near misses during one such attack.

***

Commander Hugh Winters was flat out pissed off. Since before dawn he'd been engaged in a verbal battle with the *Lexington*'s air officer over the ordnance slung under his bombers. Winters, who'd been CAG of Air Group 19 for less than a month, didn't have much political clout to throw around at this point, but he knew that they'd be going after Japanese warships later in the morning and he wanted his planes armed with AP bombs and torpedoes. The problem was that they were already armed with GP bombs in preparation for more airfield attack missions like they'd been flying for the last three weeks. The air officer refused to consider opening the magazines and re-equipping the Helldivers and TBMs.

The fight escalated into a shouting match, and finally at 0645 that morning, Winters put his request in writing. He was wasting his time. The question was bumped up to the *Lexington*'s skipper, who sided with the air officer. His first priority was the protection and safety of his ship. Opening the magazines and moving bombs and torpedoes around on the hangar deck at a time when Japanese aircraft were expected to attack was deemed too great a risk.

Frustrated, Winters felt like he was about to go hunting big game with quail shot.

Just before 1100, Winters climbed into his F6F and led his air group west toward the battleship force.

Inclement weather hampered their flight to target, and early on VB-19's Skipper Dick McGowan suffered engine trouble. He took his wingman and turned back for the *Lexington*, leaving the strike force with just ten SB2Cs. McGowan reached the *Lexington*'s task group but ditched behind a destroyer and went down with his plane.

Due to the weather, Winters was forced to take his strike—18 SB2Cs, 16 Avengers, and eight F6Fs, north over Mindoro. There, at the limit of their range, they wheeled south. Dodging storm fronts, they finally broke into the clear over the Sibuyan Sea.

Below them lay Kurita's Main Body. By this time, the *Musashi* was steaming by herself northwest, some 20 miles from the other ships. The rest of the Main Body was broken into two groups about three miles apart. To the west, Air Group 19's crews could see a pair of battlewagons flanked by two cruisers and seven destroyers. The *Essex*'s Air Group 15, which had flown along with AG-19, headed for that force. Winters led his men down on the eastern force, which included the *Yamato*, seven tin cans, and what the Americans thought were five cruisers.

The F6Fs strafed and bombed the escorts, while the TBMs released a string of GP bombs on the battleship. Bombing 19 did the same. It is probable that the crews of the *Blue Ghost* scored several near misses on the battleship *Haruna*. Hugh Winters and his fighter pilots put one bomb on the cruiser *Tone*, though little damage was done.

Meanwhile, Air Group 15, using proper anti-ship weapons, sent a 1,000-pound armor-piercing bomb down into the *Yamato*'s port anchor room. Another hit followed a few minutes later, and the enormous battlewagon shipped some 2,000 tons of water, prompting a list that took some time to counter.

Winters departed, frustrated that his men hadn't had the weapons needed to do the job properly. The next time, they would get it right.

* * *

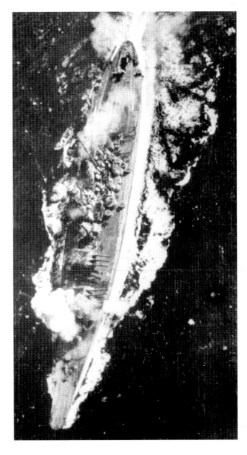

The *Yamato* fights fiercely. The super-battleship took several hits in the Sibuyan Sea that caused serious flooding. At one point, some 2,000 tons of water had poured into her hull. Rapid damage control by her crew helped keep her on an even keel and in fighting trim.

A Japanese destroyer maneuvers in support of Kurita's battleships during an attack by Air Group 13 off the *Franklin*.

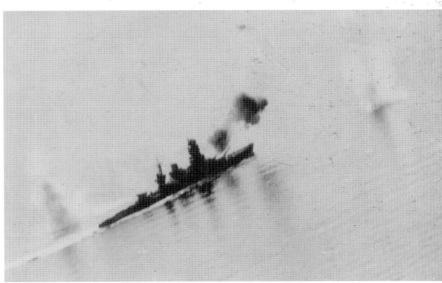

The *Nagato* fires her main gun batteries at onrushing American planes. The navy's strike aircraft were forced to fly through a 10-mile killing zone full of wildly colored flak bursts in order to carry out their attacks on Kurita's ships.

(left) The *Musashi* under attack in the afternoon of the 24th.

The American attacks continued throughout the afternoon. The *Nagato* absorbed a pair of bomb hits that knocked her speed down to 21 knots and put a main turret out of action. Four more secondary batteries were destroyed as well. Two destroyers were hit; one would sink three days later. But it was the *Musashi* that commanded most of the attention. Separated from the Main Body, with only a couple of destroyers and the cruiser *Tone* to support her defense, the super-battleship was a much easier target than the rest of Kurita's force.

Altogether, 259 American planes attacked Kurita's ships on October 24. Air Group 20 participated in the final strike on the *Musashi*. First to attack in the morning, they'd get last licks on the super-battleship to bookend their day.

Dog Smith, Air Group 20's CAG, led the strike—nine SB2Cs, eight TBMs, and a dozen F6Fs—over Samar and Masbate Islands. High over the towering cumulous clouds, they received continuous contact reports that helped guide them into the Japanese force.

Air Group 20 found a scattered fleet. *Musashi* was limping away, bleeding oil from her torpedo-riddled hull. As other air groups from the *Intrepid*, *Cabot*, *Essex*, and *Franklin* trickled onto the scene, Dog Smith led his men down against the crippled super-battleship. There was little to no cooperation between air groups.

Bombing 20 swung around from the west and put themselves up sun and to the north of the *Musashi*, even as the now-familiar but still eerie multicolored flak began to blossom around them. Meanwhile, VT-20's Avengers winged over and sped for the deck. They split up, four TBMs going for either bow. This was how it was done right—hit the target from both sides and from above.

Below them, the *Musashi* could barely maintain eight knots. She was on an even keel, battered but still full of fight.

Dog Smith dove first, leading his bombers on down through a cirrus cloud that gave his men a temporary respite from the incredible anti-aircraft fire.

Far below, the TBMs flattened out above the waves at 260 knots. They commenced their final run to target.

Down went the F6Fs, pulling ahead of the Helldivers, guns flashing, rockets sizzling off their rails. The rockets kicked up narrow, almost elegant water spouts on either side of the *Musashi*'s escorts—all misses.

(left) The heavy cruiser *Myoko* was knocked out of the battle and forced to return to Borneo after a torpedo hit damaged her propeller shafts. She's seen here from a *Franklin* torpedo bomber in the afternoon of October 24.

(left) Air Group 20, led by Commander Daniel "Dog" Smith, hammers the crippled *Musashi* with a near-perfect torpedo and dive-bombing attack. The photograph, taken around 1520 or 1530 that afternoon, shows the hits that doomed the super-battleship. In the background, rocket-firing F6Fs have near missed a destroyer. The *Musashi* sank by the bow not long after this attack.

Simultaneously, VT-20's TBMs pulled off a masterful attack. They claimed that all eight fish struck the battleship. Quite possibly, they all did hit. Japanese postwar sources relate that this last attack put 10 torpedoes into the *Musashi*, along with numerous bomb hits. Other planes from Task Group 38.2 and 38.4 made their runs around the same time and quite likely picked up a few of those torpedo hits.

However many hits the *Enterprise* planes had scored, Air Group 20 had

Bombing 20 really wanted this target. The SB2Cs stayed in their dives late, pulling out with bare feet to spare. Eighteen-thousand–pound ship-killing ‌ ‌s tumbled down around the *Musashi*. The crews claimed ‌ ‌ hits.

certainly delivered the death blows against the *Musashi*. The torpedo hits forward had decimated the ship's watertight integrity, and she began to sink by the bow. She eventually sank at 1835, taking almost half her crew with her.

(above) The last strike of the day hit the remaining battleships toward dusk. Many of the crews flew two missions that day and were exhausted. Little damage was done in this final attack.

(right) A crippled SB2C Helldiver ditches back at the American task group. Ten SB2Cs were lost on the 24th, including five from VB-18's initial attack on the *Musashi*.

(above) Exhausted flight crews relax and nap in the ready room aboard the USS Wasp. October was one of the busiest months in U.S. naval aviation history, and the constant combat wore out the aircrews.

Chapter Ten

Revenge for the *Lady Lex*

WHILE THE *MUSASHI* SUCCUMBED TO ITS DAY-LONG BEATING, AMERICAN SCOUT AIRCRAFT LOCATED ADMIRAL JISABURO OZAWA'S CARRIER FORCE TO THE NORTH OF TASK GROUP 38. Ozawa was the bait in the Japanese plan. His carriers, with barely 100 planes on their decks, were to draw the American flat-tops north, giving battleship task forces the chance to slip into Leyte Gulf and lay waste to the amphibious fleet there.

Admiral William "Bull" Halsey took the bait. Acting on the sighting reports, he massed TG-38 and steamed north, determined to take out the last of the Imperial Navy's aircraft carriers.

The battle would open at dawn on October 25, 1944, off Cape Engano, Luzon.

Deep inside the American carriers, the exhausted flight crews tried to get some sleep. For most, it was a losing proposition. They tossed fitfully, dozing for brief periods, but few were able to get the kind of rest they needed for the coming day.

(opposite) A Fighting 19 F6F Hellcat prepares to launch off the USS *Lexington* in October 1944. The Hellcat became perhaps the ultimate instrument of naval airpower by 1944. A capable strike escort and fleet air defense fighter, it also could be used to suppress airfield defenses in the fighter-bomber role. As a ship-killer, though, it was less effective. Unable to carry more than a 500-pound bomb, the F6F could not seriously damage a capital ship.

At dawn, with Admiral Marc Mitscher in tactical command, the Americans launched full deck load strikes. The Japanese hadn't been spotted yet, but everyone knew they were close. The air groups flew north with orders to orbit 50 miles out.

At 0710, search planes discovered the Japanese only 150 miles out. The radios hummed with contact reports, and the 130 aircraft already aloft turned for the reported position.

This time, Commander David McCampbell, Air Group 15's CAG, would serve as the overall strike coordinator, something the previous day's piecemeal attacks had lacked. His job was to decide which air groups would go after which targets and stay in the area to report the flow of battle back to Jimmy Flately, who served as Mitscher's talker over the radio net.

Just after 0800, the Japanese ships came into view, broken into two groups. In the lead was the Imperial Navy's last operational fleet carrier, the *Zuikaku*. She was flanked by the *Shoho*'s sister ship, *Zuiho*, and protected by two cruisers, the battleship-carrier hybrid *Ise*, and four destroyers.

Just behind this force steamed Group Six, composed of the light converted carriers *Chitose* and *Chiyoda*, escorted by another hybrid battleship, the *Hyuga*, plus a cruiser and four destroyers.

The Japanese flung massive amounts of flak at the attacking American planes. From 10 miles out, the flyers had to dodge and weave as they sought their attack positions.

Meanwhile, McCampbell assessed the situation and divvied up the targets. The air groups rolled in, and soon the Japanese were swamped by swooping dive bombers and hard-charging Avengers. Hellcats covered their approach, sizzling off rockets and pickling 500-pound bombs at the escorts.

The attack lasted about a half an hour. Air Groups 15 and 19, whose crews enjoyed a friendly rivalry, quickly smashed the light carrier *Chitose* to burning wreckage. The *Chitose* didn't last the morning through. She sank just after 0930 with 903 of her crew.

First kill: The *Chitose*, crippled by the initial strike of the day, goes down shortly after 0900 on October 25, 1944. The *Chitose* had originally been constructed as a seaplane carrier, but after the war began she was converted to a CVL. Naval intelligence identified this ship as the *Chitose* immediately after the battle, though in some postwar accounts, it has been re-identified as the *Zuiho*.

The *Chitose*'s sister ship, *Chiyoda*, was also attacked in the initial strike and endures a host of near misses, probably around 0830. She would later be crippled and left dead in the water, where a U.S. Navy cruiser task force would pick her off that evening.

In the lead group, Air Group 51 off the *San Jacinto* executed a masterful attack on the *Zuikaku* along with a few planes from the *Intrepid's* torpedo squadron. The attack put a torpedo into the big carrier's flank, knocking out its communications and causing a six-degree starboard list that greatly affected its ability to maneuver. The damage forced Ozawa to transfer his flag to the cruiser *Oyodo* at 1100 that morning.

The *Zuiho* did not escape unscathed either. At around 0831, she took a pair of bombs right on the flight deck, followed by six near misses astern in quick succession. Another near miss forward ruptured an oil tank inside her hull. She lost speed and began to list as fires spread across her deck.

McCampbell's multi-air-group attack also succeeded in hitting the light cruiser *Oyodo* with a bomb and two near misses. The light cruiser *Tama* took a torpedo hit at 0830, while a destroyer took a direct hit that sparked an enormous fire. Six minutes later, it blew up.

The day's second strike arrived about 20 minutes after the first one went home. The Americans focused on the *Chiyoda*, hitting it at 1018 with a 1,000-pound bomb that knocked her engines out. Aflame, she drifted with the current for the remainder of the day until American cruisers sunk her late that evening.

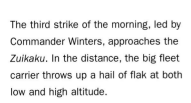

The third strike of the morning, led by Commander Winters, approaches the *Zuikaku*. In the distance, the big fleet carrier throws up a hail of flak at both low and high altitude.

One of the great ship strike photographs of military history. This shot was taken by Fighting 19's pilot Lieutenant (jg) John Hutto in his camera-equipped F6F Hellcat. Here, the *Zuikaku* endures Air Group 19's brilliant coordinated attack in the early afternoon. The white smoke streaming back from the after part of the flight deck marks the spot where VF-19's Al Seckel hit the *Zuikaku* with a 500-pound bomb.

This was Air Group 19's big chance. All morning long, Hugh Winters had fidgeted, waiting for his turn to get airborne. He'd missed the first strike, and the *Lex* didn't launch any planes for the second. The third was his. Assigned as strike coordinator, he led the *Blue Ghost*'s crews aloft at 1145. The Japanese were but 102 miles to the north. This time, it would be a short flight to target with no weather to worry about and the right ordnance in his aircraft.

This third strike was the largest of the day, with some 200 planes led by Winters and Air Group 19.

Arriving over the Japanese fleet, Winters ignored the drifting *Chiyoda*. To the north, steering northwest, the *Zuikaku* and *Zuiho* were trying their best to get away. Winters wanted the *Zuikaku*. This was the ship that had helped destroy CV-2, the original *Lady Lex*. Now, her namesake's wartime pilots would get their revenge. Winters called out targets. His boys would take care of the *Zuikaku* while Air Group 15 and the other planes from TG-38.4 went after the *Zuiho*. Winters split the *Langley*'s small group in half and sent them in after both targets.

Hugh Winters winged over and slanted down after the *Zuikaku*, his F6Fs followed by the 14 SB2Cs of VB-19. Far below, VT-19 fanned out to assail the *Zuikaku* from both sides. Here was the perfect opportunity for revenge. The *Zuikaku*, already hurt and trailing a thin slick of oil, was ripe for the kill.

But the *Zuikaku* fought back hard. Phosphorous shells exploded all around the diving American planes, and the Japanese even fired rockets up at them with metal wires attached, hoping they'd collide with them. Those Rube Goldberg concoctions didn't even slow the attackers. But the flak was more serious. In his eagerness to score, Winters stayed in his dive too long and dumped his bomb even as 25-millimeter rounds splattered around him. He took several hits, but his sturdy Hellcat kept purring. He recovered, pulled up, and took a front row seat as his men piled onto the doomed Japanese flat-top.

His Hellcat pilots scored first. Al Seckel planted his bomb just aft of the island on the flight deck. It exploded in the hangar deck, and through the rest of the attack, a ragged spire of white smoke leached from the hole in the flight deck.

A close-up of the *Zuikaku* following Air Group 19's attack. Burning from multiple bomb hits, her hull torn by torpedoes, she would roll over and sink as Hugh Winters circled overhead.

In quick succession, at least three more bombs fell upon the *Zuikaku*, setting fires and decimating the ship's fighting ability.

As near misses kicked up tremendous water spouts all around the carrier, Torpedo 19's Avengers reached their launch points in the midst of the dive-bombing attack. Already damaged, the *Zuikaku* could not hope to avoid this devastating coordinated attack. Supported by a few TBMs from the *Langley*, they pickled their fish and rolled off target. The torpedo tracks raked through the water, seen from above by at least one of the Hellcat pilots. One by one, the tracks ended alongside the *Zuikaku* and huge explosions rocked the ship and seemingly lifted it out of the water. An eye blink later, it was over. *Zuikaku*, her hull shattered by eight torpedo hits, began to roll over.

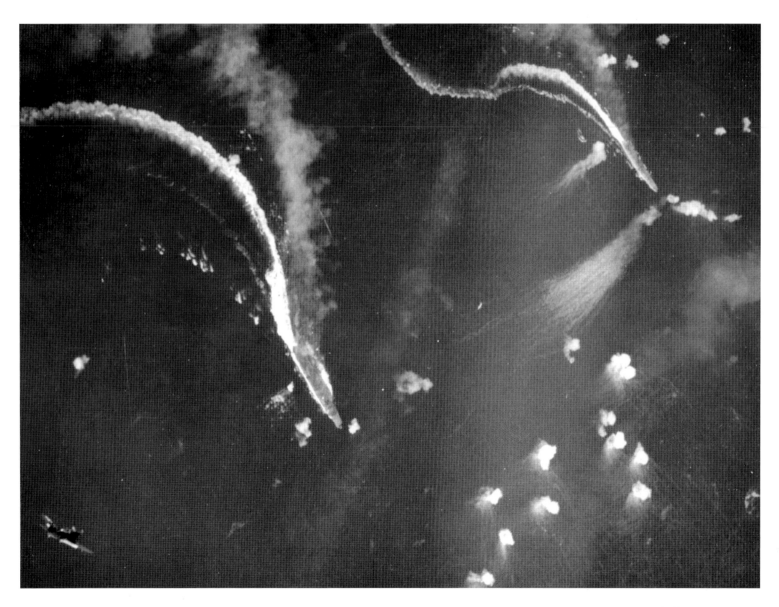

As Air Group 19 departed, The Big E's strike arrived. Winters directed Air Group 20 onto the *Zuiho*, which was still maneuvering with some effectiveness, even after the *Essex's* planes had hit her. This remarkable photo shows a VB-20 SB2C plunging onto the *Zuiho*, its dive brakes fully open.

Winters stayed overhead to coordinate the subsequent strikes. He lurked nearby, watching the *Zuikaku*'s death agonies. Ten minutes after his air group turned for home, the *Zuikaku* turned over and slipped quietly beneath the waves.

The *Blue Ghost* had avenged her namesake.

With the *Zuikaku* gone, Winters directed the subsequent attacks on the *Zuiho*. Air Group 13 off the *Franklin* attacked her next, followed by 21 planes from the *Enterprise*. Flying his second mission of the day with Air Group 20, Commander Daniel "Dog" Smith led his eager beavers in

on the surviving flat-top. The bombers swung up some before heading down into their dives. They claimed 12 hits in their furious attack, while Torpedo 20's three attacking Avengers counted two torpedoes in her side.

The *Zuiho* limped on, her crew desperately fighting to save her. It was all for naught. Deluged by bombs, torpedoes, and at least 10 near misses that caused grave damage to her hull, she skidded to a stop and sank an hour after Smith's crews had finished their runs.

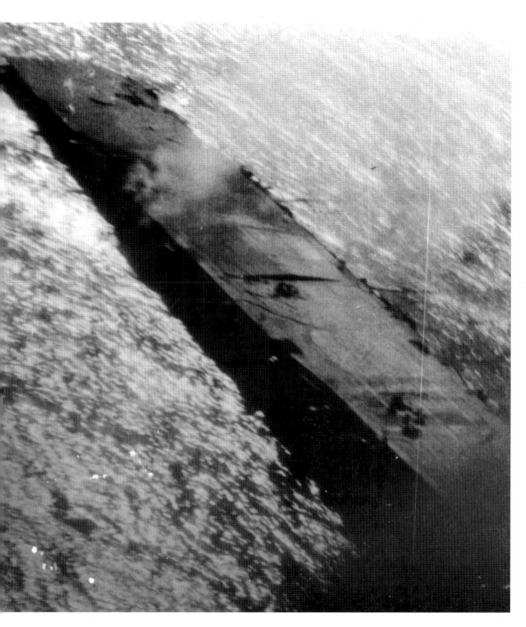

(above) The *Zuiho* twists and turns but cannot escape Air Group 20's bombing attack.

(left) Easily one of the most famous photographs of the Pacific War, this photograph of the *Zuiho* was taken from VT-20's Lieutenant (jg) Tom Armour's TBM by his crewman, Fred Rand. The *Zuiho* was mortally damaged during this attack, and it sank about an hour afterward.

(right) The *Zuiho* as seen during Air Group 20's attack from John Hutto's photo Hellcat. Hutto probably took the most dramatic photos of any carrier engagement in history. Just before he snapped this photo, 1,000-pound bomb struck the water just off the *Zuiho*'s port side.

A low-flying plane from the *Franklin*'s Air Group 13 captures the final moments of the *Zuiho*.

Throughout the afternoon, the Americans launched follow-up strikes, hoping to take out the two remaining worthwhile targets, the *Ise* and *Hyuga*. Though both ships reeled from dozens of near misses, neither ship was hit. And as the day wore on, the American strikes became smaller and less accurate. Some of the crews flew three missions that day, and by mid-afternoon exhaustion overcame everyone. One Japanese onlooker later recalled thinking that the Americans were not very good pilots, given the number of bombs that missed their targets.

(*opposite right, above, left*) The *Ise* endures a blizzard of near misses. Following the third strike of the day, most of the U.S. Navy bombers attacked the *Ise* and *Hyuga*.

(left) A Japanese destroyer fights to protect its carrier charges with all guns blazing during the action off Cape Engano.

(below) The escort carrier *Gambier Bay* burns furiously after Kurita's battleships pounded it with their massive main gun batteries.

(right) The stricken *Princeton*, hit by a lone attack D4Y "Judy" dive bomber. She was the last fleet carrier the Japanese sunk during the Pacific War. In fact, she was the last fleet carrier the U.S. Navy lost in the 20th century.

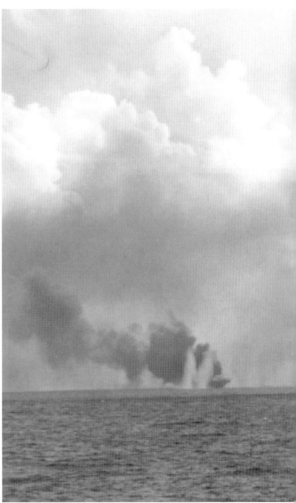

Altogether, in six distinct raids the Americans flew 527 sorties against the Japanese fleet. Two hundred of these were flown by the fighter pilots. By day's end, they had sunk four carriers and a destroyer. Perhaps they could have done better had the men been better rested, but there were a lot of celebrations across Task Group 38 that night. For Hugh Winters and his men of Air Group 19, the day was one they'd never forget. They had risen to the occasion, attacked two Japanese fleets in as many days, and had walked away the proud victors over the last of the Pearl Harbor carriers. The *Zuikaku*'s scalp would remain AG-19's

greatest achievement until another generation of naval aviators torpedoed the Hwachon Dam while serving aboard the *Princeton* during the Korean War.

In the meantime, the Japanese fleet had ceased to exist as a viable threat to the United States. Its broken elements fled the Philippines, and over the next week submarines and follow-up air strikes mopped up many of the survivors. The surviving battleships retreated to Japan, where they took refuge at Kure Harbor. In the months to come, they would be hunted down. American sea power now ruled supreme.

Part IV

1945: EXSANGUINATION

THE LAST YEAR OF THE PACIFIC WAR WAS NOTHING BUT A BLOODLETTING THAT NEED NOT HAVE HAPPENED. With the Japanese fleet neutralized, its air power crippled, its cities being burnt to cinders, and its raw material supply lines cut, there was no way Japan could avoid total defeat. Yet, the nation fought on and, in the process, tens of thousands died for a cause long since lost.

The American carriers roamed the Western Pacific, destroying a number of convoys off the coast of Indochina before turning their attention to targets on Honshu itself in February. Sweeps up to Hokkaido and back down to Kyushu wrecked much of the Japan's inter-island seagoing traffic, while a strike against the battleships and carriers in Kure Harbor hastened the demise of the last elements left to the Imperial Navy.

In one last spasm of self-destruction, the Japanese sortied the super-battleship *Yamato* against the American fleet off Okinawa in April. Caught by U.S. Navy aircraft hundreds of miles from its objective, the *Yamato* and most of her escorts succumbed to a hail of bombs and aerial torpedoes. It was a pointless waste of thousands of good men.

As the navy struck at the heart of the Empire, the 5th and 13th Air Forces worked over the remaining sea lanes between Southeast Asia and Japan. What the American submarines failed to sink, the U.S. Army Air Force destroyed. At wave-top level, B-25s and B-24s laid waste to entire convoys, leaving the ships adrift and burning, their sailors cast adrift with little hope of rescue.

In the final weeks of the war, the army air force and navy teamed up to strike at Kure Harbor again, this time sending the last of the Japanese fleet to the bottom. The conquest of air power over sea power was complete, and global warfare would forever be changed.

The U.S. Navy began 1945 with a series of devastating attacks against targets in Indochina. The raids flushed out on the last great convoys that the fast carriers were to engage during World War II. Search aircraft discovered a well-escorted group of tankers hugging the coastline. Without air cover, they didn't stand a chance. The ensuing attack destroyed the convoy and sent thousands of tons of fuel oil, desperately needed in Japan, to the bottom. This series shows the attack unfolding as seen from the USS *Hancock*'s SB2C Helldiver squadron.

By the early spring of 1945, the 5th Air Force had redeployed its medium bomber force to Luzon, where the B-25s were used against convoys off the China coast. In late March and early April, the 345th Bomb Group attacked and virtually destroyed two such convoys. In the process, they took some of the most dramatic combat photographs of the war. This series shows the convoy off Swatow, China, under attack by the Air Apaches.

(above) As the army air force launched its strikes from Luzon, the fast carriers roamed around the tattered remains of the Empire laying waste to whatever shipping its planes could find. Here, U.S. Navy aircraft catch another small convoy off the Vietnamese coast on February 18, 1845.

(above, right) In March, a lone Japanese bomber penetrated the U.S. Navy's air defenses and scored hits on the carrier *Franklin*. With a full deck load strike about to take off, the bombs wrought havoc, igniting fires and secondary explosions throughout the ship. At the cost of over 800 men, the ship was saved. Later that year, she steamed into New York Harbor under her own power.

(right) The aftermath of the kamikaze hit on the *Missouri*. The force of the impact was so great that it drove one of the Zeke's machine guns right through the barrel of a 40-millimeter anti-aircraft gun.

(above) The *Yamato* takes a near miss during a dive-bombing attack. In April, the *Yamato* sortied from southern Japan on a one-way mission to Okinawa. With its thin screen of destroyers and the light cruiser *Yahagi*, the super-battleship was supposed to fight her way through the American fleet and beach herself on Okinawa's shore, where her guns would be used in support of the garrison defending the island. It was an insane plan that ended with predictable results. American carrier planes located and destroyed the small task force before it ever got near Okinawa.

(left) The *Yamato*'s final moments, as captured by a photo plane from the USS *Yorktown* (CV-10).

The light cruiser *Yahagi* went down under a deluge of bombs, rockets, and torpedoes. Her crew never had a chance. Prior to leaving Japan, the sailors had off-loaded much of their food and distributed it to the local civilian population, which was teetering on the verge of starvation. Her captain, Tameichi Hara, had served throughout the Solomons campaign as the skipper of the legendary destroyer *Shigure*. He survived the destruction of the *Yahagi* and subsequently wrote one of the best memoirs of the Pacific War.

(above) The *Bunker Hill* aflame following a kamikaze attack in May. One of the planes struck the carrier next to the island and exploded within Air Group 84's ready rooms. The casualties were horrific.

(left) Off Hokkaido, bombers from the *Essex* caught and sank an inter-island railroad ferry. In the final months of the war, the ship-killers choked off even the coastal trade between islands in the Imperial Homeland itself.

Chapter Eleven

Pearl Harbor in Reverse

WITH NOTHING TO STOP THE AMERICAN DRIVE ACROSS THE PACIFIC, IT WAS INEVITABLE THAT JAPAN ITSELF WOULD COME UNDER MASSED AIR ATTACKS. First on the scene were the Super-Fortresses, the huge four-engined strategic bombers based out of China Burma India (CBI) and later the Marianas. Next were the carrier planes. Starting in mid-February, the fast carriers put hundreds of aircraft over targets in and around Tokyo. The Japanese responded fiercely with kamikaze attacks and conventional raids, but the carriers would not be denied.

(opposite) High over Kure Harbor, a photo recon plane, probably flown by F6F ace-in-a-day Ted Crosby, captures the climactic attack on March 19, 1945. Shore installations burn as flak fills the sky over the warships in the anchorage, some of which are already burning.

On March 19, 1945, Air Group 84 off the *Bunker Hill* spearheaded the first strike against Kure Harbor. The pilots did not lack for targets. Spread through the anchorage were the carriers *Amagi*, *Katsuragi*, and *Ryuho*; the battleships *Ise*, *Hyuga*, *Haruna*, and *Nagato*; and numerous cruisers and destroyers.

The *Wolfgang*—AG-84—led the way with its 14 TBMs, 12 Helldivers, and 19 rocket-firing Corsairs. In a swirling, low-altitude attack, the *Bunker Hill*'s crews scored hits on all three carriers, including one that blew the *Ryuho*'s number three elevator clear out of its well. Altogether, 16 ships sustained damage.

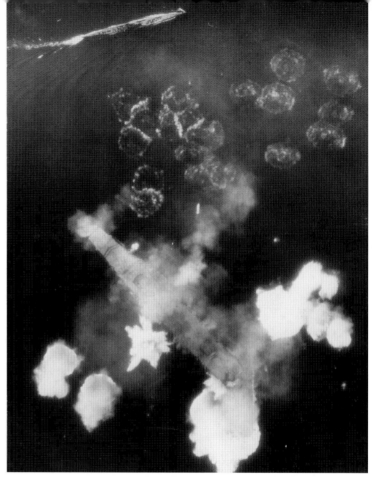

(right) Air Group 84 led the attack against Kure on the 19th. This photo was taken by VT-84's Dewey Ray just as he glide bombed the carrier *Amagi*. He scored a hit amidships, and the photo later made the cover of the navy's weekly intelligence summary magazine. Ray, who was a sports reporter prior to Pearl Harbor, contributed to the destruction of the *Amagi* and the *Yamato* in the spring of 1945. In an earlier tour in 1944 with VT-6, he helped sink the *Katori* off Truk and participated in many other ship-killing missions.

Another carrier under attack, possibly the *Katsuragi*, which was also damaged in the March 19 raid.

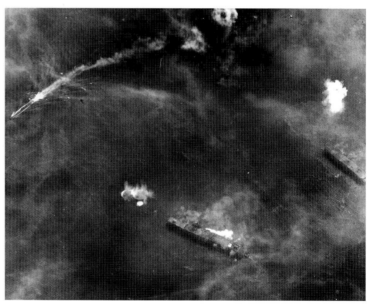

Two carriers in Kure Harbor, probably seen from Ray's TBM as he came off target. The nearest carrier is the *Amagi* with her sister ship *Katsuragi* anchored off her starboard beam. Off the *Amagi*'s bow, a Japanese submarine is under way.

The *Wolfgang* meets the *Yamato*. Air Group 84 found the *Yamato* with a head of steam up in Kure Harbor on the 19th. Here, she maneuvers to avoid a dive-bombing attack. A few weeks later, VT-84 scored at least six and possibly 10 torpedo hits on the super-battleship as she sortied for Okinawa.

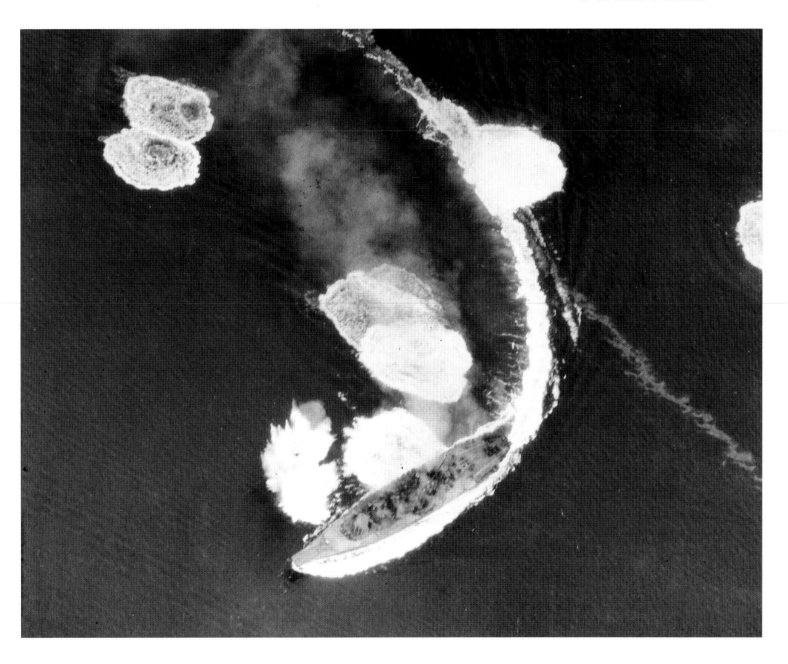

Kure Harbor soon became a magnet for further American attacks. In June, the big B-29s of the 20th Bomber Command tried to sink the *Haruna* as she lay astride a dock. Further B-29 raids followed, including several mining operations. Finally, the U.S. Navy returned at the end of July. In two devastating attacks on July 24 and July 28, 1945, the final vestiges of the Imperial Navy were destroyed from the air. *Ise*, *Hyuga*, the cruiser *Tone*, and veteran *Oyodo* all sank in the shallow harbor under an avalanche of bombs and rockets.

Three weeks later, the fighting ended.

* * *

(below) An F6F Hellcat over Kure Harbor.

(opposite) The June 22, 1945, B-29 raid on Kure. The huge bombers bracket the battleship *Haruna* with an avalanche of near misses.

The war in the Pacific has no historical parallels. It remains unique in the annals of human conflict, and chances are it will remain as such. Never before or since did aircraft play such a key role in the development of the naval campaigns that determined the course of the fighting. Almost every element of naval strategy revolved around destroying or capturing island air bases and using them as springboards for the next operation. With the capture of good fleet anchorages in the central Pacific, the American fast carriers remained forward deployed for months on end, ravaging the Japanese Empire with lightning-quick strikes.

(left) Her stern damaged by bomb hits and bleeding oil, the *Haruna* sinks at her mooring on July 28.

(opposite) In July, the U.S. Navy returned to destroy the remaining ships in Kure Harbor. These two stunning combat photos show the strike that sunk the *Haruna* on the 28th.

(right) A partially completed carrier gets worked over in Kure Harbor on July 28. This could be the *Aso*, which was about 60 percent complete when the Japanese suspended work on her in January 1945. After the July attacks on Kure, she ended her service as a test hulk for suicide weapons the Imperial Navy was frantically developing in preparation for the expected invasion of Japan.

Survivor of Leyte Gulf and the March 19 raid on Kure, the hybrid battleship *Ise*'s luck ran out in July. She sank in shallow water after a punishing series of well-executed attacks on the 28th.

In the meantime, the ship-killers of Kenney's 5th and 13th Air Forces wrecked Japan's ability to supply its forces in New Guinea and the Philippines. As the B-25s and A-20 Havocs crushed convoy after convoy, as the fast carriers hammered away in the central Pacific, and as the Silent Service's brave submariners choked off the sea lanes to and from the Imperial Homeland, Japan's war effort collapsed. The cumulative effects of the power arrayed against its army and navy became obvious by mid-1944. Japan's soldiers, isolated in remote Pacific jungles, starved. In some cases, they resorted to cannibalism to survive. Unable to supply their troops, unable to bring them home, the largest concentrations of Imperial Army units—in New Guinea and the Philippines—died on the vine. It was a triumph of combined air-sea power, and the strategy saved tens of thousands of Allied lives.

The Pacific War turned on a few events in the opening months of the war. From December 1941 through the spring of 1943, the entire flow of the conflict between Japan and the United States was dictated by the ship-killers. The Japanese set the tone at Pearl Harbor when they destroyed the American battle line. With only the carriers remaining, the navy was forced to use them as their primary weapons to counterattack the Japanese. That set the stage for the confrontation in the Coral Sea.

And there in May 1942, the few hits scored by Bill Ault and his comrades from the *Yorktown* ensured the *Shokaku* would not be at Midway. Had Ault and Powers not pressed their attack to such a self-sacrificial extreme, Spruance could have faced five or even six flat-tops in June, not four. The great victory at Midway was set up by the dive bomber pilots of Coral Sea.

Ise's sister ship, *Hyuga*, fell victim to U.S. Navy aircraft four days earlier. Here she lies on the bottom of Kure Harbor.

A strike recon photo captures the *Hyuga*'s destruction. She's seen here surrounded by fuel oil that has spilled from her ruptured tanks.

The *Ise* sitting on the harbor bottom after the July 28 attacks. The amount of oil fouling the harbor after the U.S. Navy strikes must have posed an enormous environmental problem.

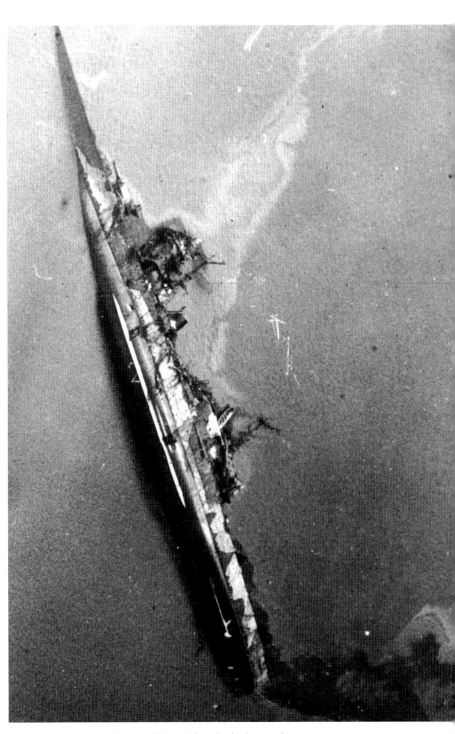

On the 28th, Ozawa's flagship at the end of Cape Engano drew the wrath of diving Helldivers and TBMs. Here, she's straddled by near misses even as at least one bomb strikes home, kicking up a huge cloud of smoke, flames, and debris.

Her hull shattered, the *Oyodo* rolled over into the harbor mud.

It was the *Tone*'s turn next. Veteran of almost every fleet engagement of the Pacific War, U.S. Navy planes secured her destruction at the end of July in her home anchorage.

The offensive at Guadalcanal finally wrested the initiative away from the Japanese. The Imperial Navy lost many valuable ships during the fighting that summer and fall, including the carrier *Ryuho* and battleships *Hiei* and *Kirishima*. More important, the raging battles off Guadalcanal destroyed the Imperial Navy's best weapon—its carrier-based air groups. After Santa Cruz, the Japanese aircrew quality declined so precipitously that they never again were able to launch a coordinated attack against an American capital ship.

(*right and previous page*) Based on the *Hiryu*'s design and slated to become the next-generation carrier for the Kido Butai, the *Katsuragi* wasn't finished until Ozawa's force at Leyte Gulf had been destroyed. With no remaining carrier air groups left, the big carrier became little more than a bomb and rocket magnet for attacking U.S. Navy aircraft. These four photographs are a testament to the finality of Japan's naval defeat in the Pacific. Bereft of planes, sitting helpless in her own anchorage, she was pounded where she lay, unable even to get up steam in her own defense.

The following year, Ed Larner, John Henebry, and the surprisingly small band of innovators from the 5th Bomber Command transformed the entire New Guinea campaign with their knock-out blow in the Bismarck Sea. The destruction of that Lae-bound convoy compromised Japan's ability to supply its forces in eastern New Guinea. More important, for the first time in the war, Allied land-based airpower had proven superior to the Imperial Navy. No longer could the Japanese sail ships into land-based bomber range in the SWPA and expect to escape unscathed. Indeed, more often than not, their convoys were simply wiped out.

By 1944 and 1945, massed air attacks against American warships almost always resulted in catastrophic losses to the Japanese squadrons. Lone snipers became the only real danger—the few crews who somehow penetrated the American air defenses to launch courageous, and usually fatal, solo attacks against the fast carriers. The *Princeton* was destroyed in this manner, and the *Franklin* very nearly so the following year. In the meantime, the Americans crushed every attempt by the Imperial Navy to slow the inexorable drive toward the homeland. Its fleet shattered by the fall of 1944, Japan turned to kamikaze attacks as a means to stem the tide. Though they caused considerable damage, the kamikazes failed to break the choke-hold that encircled Japan by early 1945.

In the final months of the war, the American ship-killers hunted down the broken remnants of the Japanese fleet. Few survived the onslaught. Those that did were quickly disposed of in the Bikini atomic bomb tests or simply scrapped. Never in modern history has one nation's navy and merchant marine been as completely destroyed as Japan's.

The ship-killers made the difference. Facing daunting odds, they pressed their attacks through storms of flak and swirling fighters to destroy the ships within which the hopes of nations rode. At war's end, their duty done, the survivors returned home and disappeared into anonymity. Few wrote published memoirs, and even fewer writers sought them out to tell their stories for them. And yet, this handful of gallant men helped shape the events of their day with an influence that defied their small number.

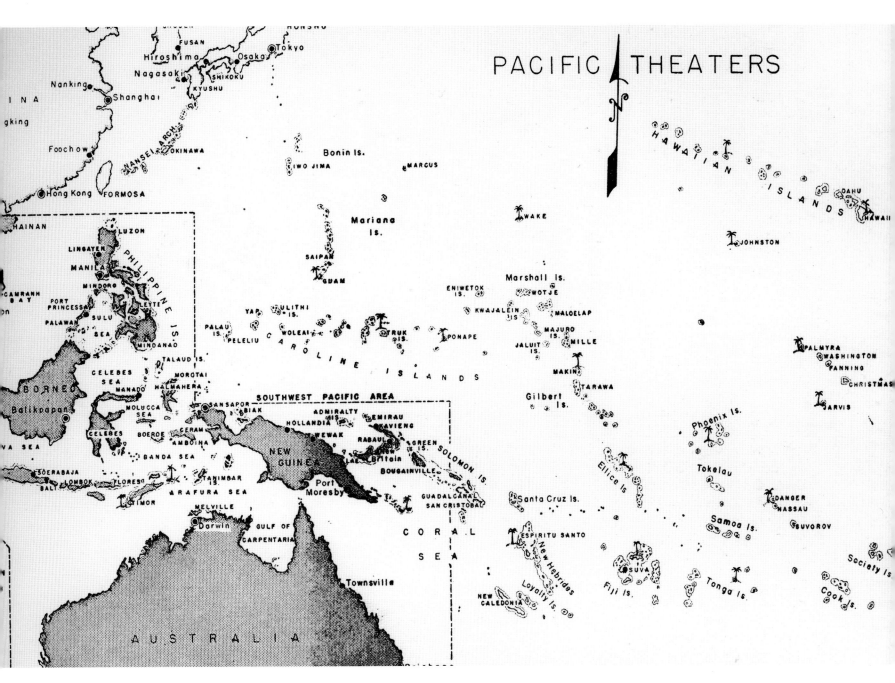

The southwest Pacific theater. *Jungle Ace*

Index

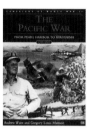
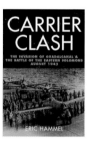

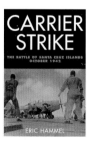